DOO WOP

THE MUSIC, THE TIMES, THE ERA

by "Cousin Brucie" Morrow
with Rich Maloof

FOREWORD BY NEIL SEDAKA

INTRODUCTION BY TJ LUBINSKY

PRODUCED BY BAND-F LTD.

STERLING

New York / London
www.sterlingpublishing.com

STERLING and the distinctive Sterling logo are registered trademarks of Sterling Publishing Co., Inc.

Library of Congress Cataloging-in-Publication Data
Morrow, Cousin Bruce.
Doo wop : the music, the times, the era / Bruce Morrow with Rich Maloof ; foreword by Neil Sedaka.
p. cm.
ISBN-13: 978-1-4027-4276-7
ISBN-10: 1-4027-4276-2
1. Doo wop (Music)--History and criticism. I. Maloof, Rich. II. Title.
ML3527.M67 2007
2007004642

2 4 6 8 10 9 7 5 3

Published by Sterling Publishing Co., Inc.
387 Park Avenue South, New York, NY 10016

First Edition

Distributed in Canada by Sterling Publishing
c/o Canadian Manda Group, 165 Dufferin Street
Toronto, Ontario, Canada M6K 3H6
Distributed in the United Kingdom by GMC Distribution Services
Castle Place, 166 High Street, Lewes, East Sussex, England BN7 1XU
Distributed in Australia by Capricorn Link (Australia) Pty. Ltd.
P.O. Box 704, Windsor, NSW 2756, Australia

Produced by BAND-F Ltd.
F-Stop Fitzgerald, President
Karen Jones, Director of Development
Mie Kingsley, Managing Editor
David Perry, Design Director

Design by David Perry and Jason Cring

Printed in China
All rights reserved

Sterling ISBN-13: 13: 978-1-4027-4276-7
ISBN-10: 1-4027-4276-2

For information about custom editions, special sales, premium and
corporate purchases, please contact Sterling Special Sales
Department at 800-805-5489 or specialsales@sterlingpub.com.

For Jodie,
thank you so much for
the beautiful music
of our life together.

And to all of the Doo Wop fans
throughout the world.
This memory is dedicated
especially to you.

TABLE OF CONTENTS

Foreword
by Neil Sedaka

For as long as I can remember, music has been my passion. Though I began studying piano at the Julliard School of Music at age nine and had every intention of becoming a classical pianist, Bach and Beethoven were not the ticket to being in the "in crowd" at Abraham Lincoln High School in Brooklyn, New York. That would come one afternoon after school while sitting in Andrea's Pizza Parlor in Brighton Beach listening to "Earth Angel" by the Penguins playing on the jukebox. I had always enjoyed harmony singing but knew instantly that this was different. It was exciting, teen-oriented and had a natural, spontaneous sound.

That was the moment I became hooked on the sweet laments and four-part harmonies of doo-wop.

A few classmates and I quickly got together and formed our own group, the Linc-Tones, performing at local hops, TV shows, bar mitzvahs and weddings. We later changed our name to the Tokens when the New York City subway system moved from nickels to tokens (yes, at one time you could ride from Brooklyn to the Bronx for a nickel!). We had a few local hits together, but I left to pursue a career as a solo artist, something I have enjoyed tremendous success with to this day. Back then, however, radio play and selling records went hand in hand, with disc jockeys ruling the airwaves. Fortunately there was one guy "in the know" on the music scene who actively supported fresh new talent. That person was the legendary "Cousin" Bruce Morrow.

I first met Cousin Brucie in 1958 when he was putting together one of his famous teenage hops. I had just released my first solo record The Diary which he enthusiastically played, giving me added support and exposure. We hit it off instantly. We have often discussed that it might be because we were both Brooklynites and of a certain breed, just like Neil Diamond, Carole King, Barbra Streisand and the many other artists who emerged from this fabled borough. Our parents insisted we become accomplished and successful, so Cousin Brucie and I were both driven, ambitious, disciplined and achieved success at an early age. There were a few disc jockeys who had shady backgrounds, but Brucie was wholesome, honest and almost childlike in his enthusiasm for the business. We eventually ended up living in the same apartment complex on Ocean Parkway for a period, taking our kids to the rides at Coney Island and for hot dogs at Nathan's. In all my travels, one thing remains true: No matter where you go, Brooklyn stays with you.

Fifty years later I still enjoy listening to doo wop with its high falsetto, deep predominant bass and simple yet emotional teenage laments. I can think of no better music industry icon to bring doo wop to life for readers of this book than Cousin Bruce Morrow. He was there at the beginning as an innovator, started many young artists on their careers, and to this day is a consummate communicator.

—Neil Sedaka

For over fifty years, Neil Sedaka has written, performed and produced countless songs including "Where the Boys Are," "Oh! Carol," "Calendar Girl," "Breaking Up is Hard to Do," "Love Will Keep Us Together" and "Solitaire." He has a star on the Hollywood Walk of Fame and is a member of the Songwriters Hall of Fame, where he has also been honored with the Sammy Cahn Lifetime Achievement award.

BOMP BOMP BA
DANG A DONG
DING / BOME
BOME BOME DO
DO BOP / PAPA
COW PAPA COW
PAPA COW COW /
DIDDLE LITTLE LIT LIT
LIT YEAH / DUN
DUN DUN DUN
DUN DUN DUN

Introduction
by TJ Lubinsky

WHAT IS DOO WOP?

Although in some ways doo wop is in the eye of the beholder, it is a vocal styling which personifies the emotions and special feelings that let us "Remember Then." It's that music in our hearts that we will never forget: the melodies and memories of being young, falling in love and teenage angst.

As Cousin Brucie has said many times on our PBS specials, doo wop is the soundtrack of our lives, the backbeat to every important rite of passage. Those songs of the past allow us to connect emotionally, physically and spiritually with our wives, husbands, girlfriends, boyfriends, dream girls, fantasies, friends and family. They are our connection to innocence, songs that express our true feelings and which help us say what's in our hearts.

If nothing else, "doo wop" is a term that has redefined a blending of classic rhythm and blues with vocal group harmonies, street corner singers, falsetto leads, baritone and bass singers whose deep voices could simulate any musical instrument. Take the tender sounds and angelic voices created by Rudy West and the Five Keys crooning "The Glory of Love" and "Wisdom of a Fool," or Willy Winfield and the Harptones' melancholic yet inspiring "That's the Way

it Goes,""My Memories of You" and "The Masquerade Is Over."

Doo wop is "Big City USA" music from the founding fathers of the 1950s R&B vocal harmony, such as the timeless polished harmonies of "Golden Tear Drops," "I Only Have Eyes for You" and "Mia Amore" from the Windy City's Flamingos. It's the blow harmony *d-hoo* phrasing of Cleveland's Bobby Lester, or Harvey Fuqua and the Moonglows' veritable bible of romance "The Ten Commandments of Love" and "Sincerely." It's Los Angeles' Cleve Duncan and the Penguins bringing back those "Memories of El Monte" and their anthem "Earth Angel."

Other cities represented were Pittsburgh, whose Jimmy Beaumont and the Skyliners gave up plans, dreams, hopes and schemes in "Since I Don't Have You" and "This I Swear." The Students, from Cincinnati, expressed their frustrations with a society telling them they are "So Young." Philly legends Lee Andrews and the Hearts related "Long, Lonely Nights" and "Tear Drops" from a love gone awry; and Brooklyn's own Tough Tony (aka Little Anthony) with the Imperials started anew with "Tears on My Pillow" and "Two Kinds of People in the World." Two kinds, indeed: the

My personal love for doo wop came from listening to Cousin Brucie play these songs.

ones who love real music (i.e., doo wop) and the ones who don't get what it is that we doo wop lovers share.

In the early 1960s, the doo wop sound evolved with many of the Big Apple's white vocal groups paying tribute to the founding fathers of R&B. I fantasize about what it must have felt like to be with "The Cuz" at Palisades Park, onstage at the Brooklyn Paramount, the New York Paramount or the Albee, even about having a hot dog at Nathan's with your "Coney Island Baby" for the first time.

New York's late 1950s/early 1960s doo wop is represented by Lenny Cocco and the Chimes bringing back the standards of yesteryear; Nicky Santo and the Capris proclaiming "There's a Moon Out Tonight"; Johnny Maestro and the Crests singing "16 Candles" every time we have a birthday; Jimmy Gallagher and the Passions longing "Just to Be with You"; and from Jersey City, the Duprees' spine-tingling "Have You Heard" and "You Belong to Me."

Let's not forget those fun, up-tempo dance records like the Silhouettes' "Get a Job," the Solitaires' "Walking Along" and the Del Vikings' "Come Go With Me." Or, at the other end of the spectrum, slow dancing to Hal Miller and the Rays serenading about two "Silhouettes" on the shade; Pookie Hudson and the Spaniels saying "Goodnight Sweetheart Goodnight" at three o'clock in the morning; Purkle Lee Moses and the El Dorados wondering is it yes or is it no on "I'll Be Forever Loving You"; the Mello-Kings crooning "Tonite, Tonite"; and of course, the great Fred Parris along with the Five Satins singing the all time number one doo wop anthem "In the Still of the Nite."

My personal love for and attraction to doo wop came from listening to Cousin Brucie play these songs on WCBS-FM. I remember it like it was yesterday: growing up in Bradley Beach on the Jersey Shore, being fifteen years old, discovering the music for the first time and discovering myself in the process. Every time I hear a doo wop record, I'm brought instantly back to those moments.

By the time I reached my teens, though, they were called "oldies." But to me, they were "newies" throughout this amazing journey of discovery. The songs and their

SCENE FROM CARNIVAL ROCK

THE PLATTERS IN THE GIRL CAN'T HELP IT

messages are timeless. The lyrics, melodies and harmonies helped me identify and shape my personal values: honesty, integrity and appreciation for the love of my wife, daughter and family.

More than any other style of music, doo wop had a profound effect on my life. It formed my desire to be back in time when those sounds were first created and to help preserve, respect and share the history of the original performers who define rock 'n' roll. Yes, it happened later for me—I was born in 1972—but it gave me that same feeling as those countless teens who had grown up in America in the 1950s and early 1960s. I was able to experience those feelings because the music was still being played then, as it is today. And because great doo wop songs, regardless of era, are pure and honest, something we all feel and share at our core, regardless of age, religion, race or culture.

These songs have an honest and open form: boy meets girl, boy and girl fall in love, boy and girl walk down the aisle, boy and girl start a life, start a family and have a boy and girl of their own. The music explained to us the things our parents could not and shaped our hopes for the future. It was the music of adolescence ushering us into adulthood, meaningfully teaching us lessons of life and "Who Wrote the Book of Love."

The songs were every kid's guide to psychology and anatomy and helped us grow up into responsible, proper, respectful adults. The music helped us get in touch with our inner feelings and expressed in a "cool" way what was going on with our emotions and hormones. The songs always left us feeling good at the core, positive and hopeful about the world around us and the world ahead of us.

So what is doo wop?

Whether it's the Marcels' Fred Johnson's (aka Mr. Bassman) *bomp bomp ba dang a dong ding* from "Blue Moon" or the Five Discs' *bome, bome, bome bome do do bop* on "Never Let You Go," or Frankie Lymon and the Teenagers' *oodly papa cow papa cow papa cow cow* on "I Promise To Remember," or the Cleftones' "Little Girl of Mine" (*diddle little lit lit lit, yeah*), or Dion and the Belmonts belting out "I Wonder Why" (*dun dun dun dun dun dun dun dun dun dun dun*) or my personal favorite, "Here Am I Broken Hearted" by the Four J's, doo wop is a feeling.

It's that feeling we get, from the roots of R&B in the cities to Vinny's pizza shop in Da Bronx. It's the songs that make us feel good, songs that make us want to sing along and songs that have a special place in our hearts and our life's journey. It comes every time we hear a classic record, which takes us back to every Saturday night with Cousin Brucie on WABC (and now on Sirius Satellite Radio). Doo wop is the music, the artists, the songs…and especially "the Cuz." It is our portal back to those moments in time—our personal time machine to youth and innocence.

I pray that my nineteen-month-old daughter Kaitlyn and her generation (and whatever they'll be calling music by then) will understand the power and magical feeling we could only get from hearing Eugene Mumford or Billy Ward and the Dominoes touching us with "Star Dust," and what exactly that "feeling" was.

Doo wop is…our lives, our souls and our music.

Thank you, Cousin Brucie, for helping me learn the importance of these connections in this world we share, and for helping to shape the music and memories of our lives. You and the groups have profoundly and permanently affected our lives.

"Sincerely," (pun intended)
TJ Lubinsky

TJ Lubinsky is creator and executive producer of the CD / DVD compilations Doo Wop 50, Doo Wop 51, *and* Rock, Rhythm and Doo Wop. *He is also host of Doo Wop Gold on Sirius Satellite Radio and frequently appears with Cousin Brucie on PBS specials.*

BACK IN THE DAY: "COUSIN BRUCIE" AT ONE OF HIS LEGENDARY PALISADES AMUSEMENT PARK WEEKEND STAGE SHOWS. DIG THAT LEOPARD SKIN TUXEDO!

Preface
by "Cousin Brucie" Morrow

This book has been living within me, growing along with me, for nearly five decades. It took shape slowly as my generation matured and as rock 'n' roll music grew into its own shoes.

Unlike an encyclopedia, a music guide or a traditional account of history, this is a record of emotions and experiences. I see it as a collection of reflections, each of them a meaningful moment not only in my own life but in the lives of hundreds of artists and thousands of music fans.

The way I hear it, doo wop represents a chapter in the story of our lives. I hope you'll find your personal story somewhere in these pages. Read on and relive our memories, our times.

"Cousin Brucie" Morrow
2007

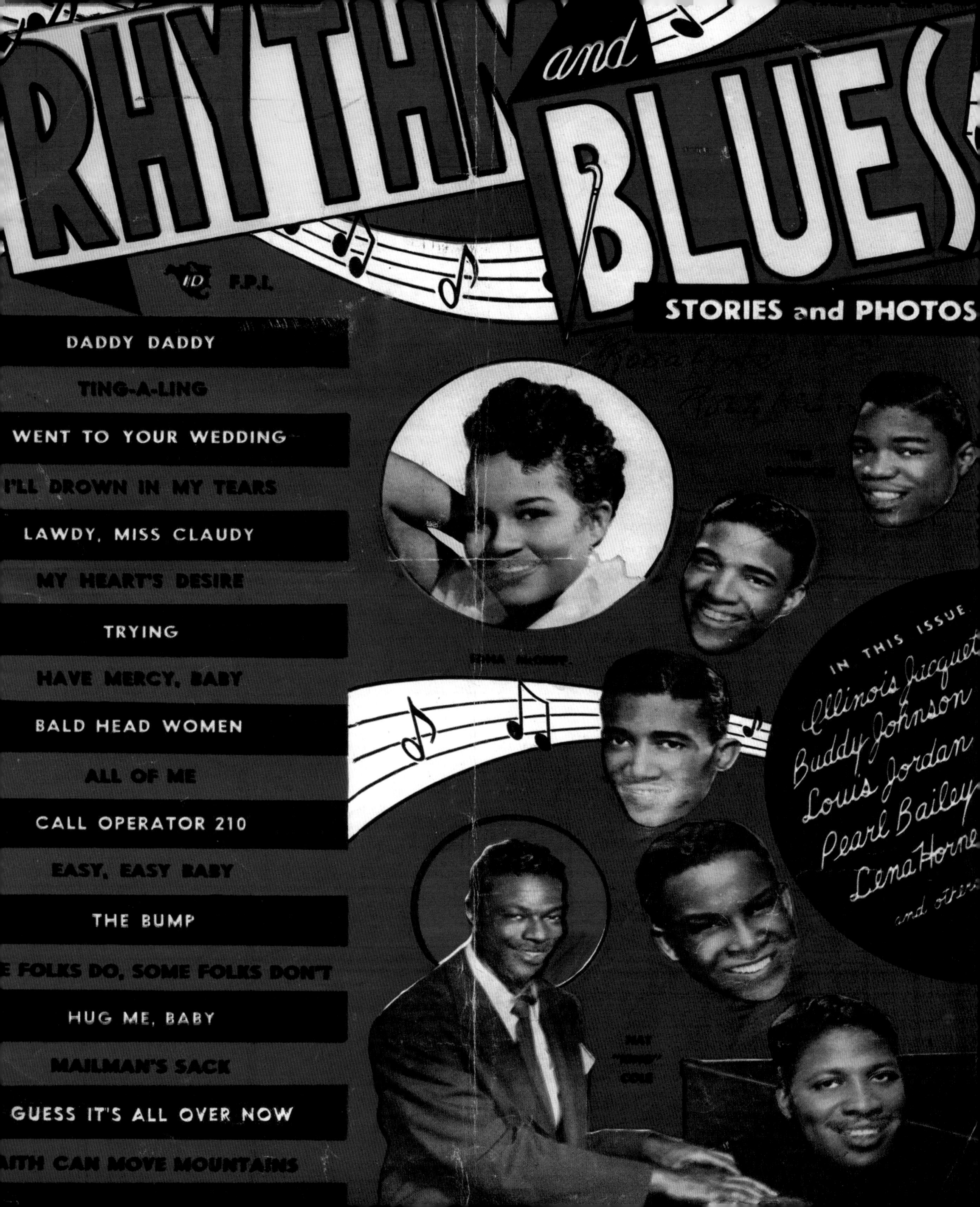
RHYTHM and BLUES
F.P.I.
STORIES and PHOTOS
DADDY DADDY
TING-A-LING
WENT TO YOUR WEDDING
I'LL DROWN IN MY TEARS
LAWDY, MISS CLAUDY
MY HEART'S DESIRE
TRYING
HAVE MERCY, BABY
BALD HEAD WOMEN
ALL OF ME
CALL OPERATOR 210
EASY, EASY BABY
THE BUMP
E FOLKS DO, SOME FOLKS DON'T
HUG ME, BABY
MAILMAN'S SACK
GUESS IT'S ALL OVER NOW
AITH CAN MOVE MOUNTAINS
IN THIS ISSUE
Illinois Jacquet
Buddy Johnson
Louis Jordan
Pearl Bailey
Lena Horne
and other

CHAPTER 1

Africa to America

Everyone enjoys the simple pleasure of a good song. We hum along, sing out the lines we know and love, and maybe do a little dance. The stories within the lyrics, whether they're happy or sad, tell the stories within our own hearts.

Like all great popular music, that's what doo wop is all about. But I can't in good conscience start talking about doo wop without acknowledging where the stories came from in the first place. Ethically, I must start deep down, where the roots of this music first took hold. So, a history lesson is in order. I'd like to ask everybody to sit back and listen to Professor Cousin Brucie for a few moments, and by the time we're finished I think you'll start listening to music very differently.

In many ways, music today is what it has always been: an expression of one person's experience with the power to resonate with the entire world. Sure, we do our listening today on digital compact discs, and songs can be beamed to your cell phone or portable radio from a satellite 250 miles above the Earth. But the music—the core experience—is the same in this digital era as it was when the first caveman started beating on a hollow log with his club. Music is communication and self-expression and storytelling. It's a record of the human experience.

So let's start at the beginning. Imagine a caveman just coming in from a hard day out with the other Cro-Magnons. His pal Thong was eaten by a saber-toothed tiger, but otherwise, this guy had a pretty good day. He led the hunt and bagged a woolly mammoth. Back in the warmth of his cave, he looks at his woman, his paintings on the wall and the fire he built without so much as a Zippo stick. He's

Music is communication and self-expression and storytelling. It's a record of the human experience.

bursting with pride. So what does he want to do? He wants to shout out and tell the story about how great he is. He wants to sing.

I caught me a big mammal
And made a fire out of wood
Yeah, I'm so fertile all the cavegirls love me
But I don't smell that good.

Something like that! I know they weren't too sharp with the lyrics back then, but that was the idea: to tell a story, maybe embellish it with a little imagination and share it.

The voice was the first instrument, and from the start music was the story of our experience —a way to express the human condition, whatever our condition may be at the time. There in his cave, our caveman wanted to sing his own praises and let the local cave community know how great he was for catching next week's dinner. He wants Mrs. Caveman, all his children, and the people in the cave next door to appreciate his value and worth. I think that's what the first singing was driven by: expressing the I and telling stories about life as we lived it.

The feeling of self-worth that you get from singing a song—even someone else's song—is contagious. We all need approval and we look for ways to express our hardships and victories, our ups and downs, so that someone might say, "I hear you. I feel the same way. Thank you for saying it." The caveman's song might be about getting chased by some lions while someone today might sing about chasing skirts. With or without words, music and expression grow out of the feelings and experiences in life that we all share. That's why the experience very quickly transfers from the *I* to the *We*. Everyone gravitates toward the musical expression. Pretty soon everyone is reporting or replaying their stories in song.

Torn from Mother Africa

Of course, there's no accurate record of what early man did from day to day, aside from the tales told in wall paintings. But we do know what Westerners saw in the ancient cultures they found

The feeling of self—worth that you get from singing a song is contagious.

eons later on the Gold Coast of Africa. From the early 1600s to the late 1800s, Western ships sailed to the west coast of Africa—what is now Senegal, Guinea, Nigeria, Sierra Leone, and the Congo—to pursue one of the worst nightmares of humanity: the slave trade.

It baffles me that the slave traders saw and even appreciated the rich culture of the Africans they were about to enslave, and still they destroyed these lives, families and communities. In 1817, a man from London took these notes about a huge communal dance he witnessed in Ashanti (what is now Ghana):

…More than a hundred bands burst at once on our arrive, [all playing] the peculiar airs of their several chiefs; the horns flourished their defiances, with the beating of innumerable drums and metal instruments, and then yielded for a while to the soft breathings of their long flutes, which were truly harmonious; and a pleasing instrument, like a bagpipe without the drone, was happily blended. [1]

All the basic elements of music as we enjoy it today were there in African music over four-hundred years ago. Not that the music itself was basic; their complex rhythms would be enough to make a modern drummer dizzy. Africans had a sophisticated array of instruments, including bells, gongs, rattles, animal-hide drums, wood flutes, horns made from elephant tusks, and even some stringed instruments. They played contagious rhythms under catchy melodies and sang lyrics about their lives.

Music was the newspaper of their time, with headline stories of love and of war. There was a

When we share our ideas and help complete someone else's, the creative dream comes alive.

All the basic elements of music as we enjoy it today existed in African music over four-hundred years ago.

When we share our ideas
and help complete
someone else's,
the creative dream
comes alive.

The feeling of self-worth that you get from singing a song is contagious.

eons later on the Gold Coast of Africa. From the early 1600s to the late 1800s, Western ships sailed to the west coast of Africa—what is now Senegal, Guinea, Nigeria, Sierra Leone, and the Congo—to pursue one of the worst nightmares of humanity: the slave trade.

It baffles me that the slave traders saw and even appreciated the rich culture of the Africans they were about to enslave, and still they destroyed these lives, families and communities. In 1817, a man from London took these notes about a huge communal dance he witnessed in Ashanti (what is now Ghana):

…More than a hundred bands burst at once on our arrive, [all playing] the peculiar airs of their several chiefs; the horns flourished their defiances, with the beating of innumerable drums and metal instruments, and then yielded for a while to the soft breathings of their long flutes, which were truly harmonious; and a pleasing instrument, like a bagpipe without the drone, was happily blended. [1]

All the basic elements of music as we enjoy it today were there in African music over four-hundred years ago. Not that the music itself was basic; their complex rhythms would be enough to make a modern drummer dizzy. Africans had a sophisticated array of instruments, including bells, gongs, rattles, animal-hide drums, wood flutes, horns made from elephant tusks, and even some stringed instruments. They played contagious rhythms under catchy melodies and sang lyrics about their lives.

Music was the newspaper of their time, with headline stories of love and of war. There was a song for most every event in their lives, whether it was celebrating the birth of a child, preparing for battle, praising the spirits for a healthy crop, greeting newcomers or cheering a sporting event. If you grew a new tooth, they had a song for it!

Many eyewitnesses said that West Africans played their music with an entire tribe gathered in a circle. There's comfort in a circle for all of us. That's how children in nursery schools learn about music, sitting around facing one another. In the safety of a circle we have a setting for exchanging experiences and developing relationships. That's what music is all about. In fact, that is music. When we share our ideas and help complete someone else's, the creative dream comes alive.

There in the jungle, they even had call-and-response songs just like the ones we sing along to at concerts. A leader, like some indigenous rock star, would sing a line and a group of people would gather to sing the refrain.

My horse is as tall as a high wall
Oh, the broad spears!
He will fight against ten—he fears nothing
Oh, the broad spears! [2]

The foundation of rhythmic music—of rock 'n' roll—was all in place. These were the first strands of our musical DNA.

This is why it's so unbelievable that they tore these people from their families, brutally shackled them in chains and shipped them like cargo in the hulls of ships. What a nightmare. Can you imagine the frustration—the anger? Anger is such a pure form of emotion, and with all that emotional energy, the creative process burns. The slave traders didn't know it, or didn't care, but with this disgraceful treatment of fellow human beings, they were igniting these huge flames. They were creating nuclear reactors. There's no question in my mind that later music like doo wop and rock 'n' roll was stoked in the fires of the early black experience. In one way or another, it's still there in every song.

All that passion and anger and longing has to come out somewhere. When people suffer, they react. You can bind arms and legs, but you can never chain up someone's heart.

Unbound Souls

The history of American slavery was first written in song. Through the oral tradition of music, real human experience can be expressed in a way that goes far beyond what anyone could say with the written word. Just like the lessons in the Bible or the ancient Greek tales in Homer's *Odyssey*, stories within slave songs were retold thousands of times, and they constantly evolved depending on who was telling the story and what his or her personal experience was. The voices changed, but what always remained somewhere in there was the seed of truth. That's a very powerful thing. Undeniable, inescapable truth is what made slave songs resonate so strongly.

In slave songs, it was a sad truth. Every type of music owes a debt to the music that came before it, and the songs of American slaves were steeped in traditions of the African homeland. How tragic, though, that Mother Africa's songs of celebration, community and joy were reborn across the ocean as mourning, alienation and pain. Once there were chants and drumming and dancing within the safety of a tribal circle; now there were lonely solos from a solitary worker among the crop rows.

I've always felt that music is a wonderful balm. It soothes our wounds. A happy song can make your whole body feel good, but even a sad song is a way to start healing because it provides a way to express yourself and get the feeling out. Plus, it's a way of reaching out to someone else for help. I was thinking of this when I learned about field hollers (sometimes called "cornfield hollers" or "water calls"), which are the mournful cries that a lone slave would sing to the sky. They could be cries for water, or for help, or for salvation. What's really amazing is that the field hollers would be answered; another slave in a far-away field would hear the song and repeat the melody back across the plantation. Sometimes several slaves would pick up the same melody and sing to one another across acres of cotton or corn. It's as if they were reaching across incredible distances to the next hand in a tribal circle. Field hollers are such a great example of music's healing power and its ability to connect people.

It wasn't all lonesome wailings and worksongs. Slaves mastered a variety of instruments, which were often handed down by the children of white families, and played recreationally to relax, celebrate happier moments and unite their own families. Documents dating back to the late 1600s report that black musicians played banjos, violins, French horns and flutes for holiday celebrations and balls hosted by their white owners. One owner described a lullaby sung by a slave in loving terms: "I did not know his song but he sang with such richness, such sobriety and ease, that I felt a warming in my heart."[3]

I see moments like these as bright spots in an otherwise dark time. In a small but really important way, these were the first examples of black culture and white culture coming together. Music paved the pathway for that. When a black man played fiddle at a dance or sang songs for a Christmas dinner, he was providing the soundtrack to the white man's life. And black slaves were known to give music lessons to white children, so you can see how the next generation would be a little better connected than the one before because they shared something special. Music provided a link that hadn't been there before. There was reason to believe, even back then, that blacks and whites could be united through the brotherhood of music.

A song and a prayer

If you trace the history of hip-swaying, foot-stomping rock 'n' roll, you'll find it leads directly back to the church. How's that for irony? The truth is that "black" music really came into its own in the rear pews of eighteenth-century chapels where black people sang their hearts out. Way back in the 1730s, during a religious movement known as the Great Awakening, people started singing religious songs, or hymns, instead of simply putting scripture to music. Hymns had their origin

in Europe, but in the voice of a black American they truly became soulful. Think of that word, soulful—literally, full of soul. Longing for an answer from above as to why their lives were so full of pain and difficulty, black communities found in church music a true soul salvation.

In times of deep trouble, such as when the storm clouds of war begin to gather, people tend to turn to God. Around the time of the Civil War (1861--1865) you could hear the saber-rattling all across our young country, and spiritual singing was a source of comfort within rural, southern congregations. Taken on the road by touring evangelists, spirituals sowed the seeds of gospel music, which emerged in more urban settings. To my ears, spiritual music has a sound that is down-

to-earth and soul-searching, like what we would hear years later in the blues. Gospel, on the other hand, is loose and free, full of hand-clapping and jubilant urges to give yourself over to the Lord.

In all black churches there was a gospel tradition called "The Shout." Following a prayer service, all the benches would be pushed back against the walls and the congregation would form a big circle. They'd stomp their feet, dance, sing and go into these wild chants. Shouts were like an American equivalent of the tribal circles back in Africa. The music must have been fantastic.

When the prayers within slave songs were at last answered by the Emancipation Proclamation (1863), black musicians gained the freedom to travel and perform. One of the first groups to

tour was the Fisk Jubilee Singers, a group of folk singers from the famed Fisk University in Nashville, Tennessee. The Jubilees spread their spiritual sound while setting themselves well apart from traveling minstrel troupes. Minstrel shows, featuring a mix of music and comedy, pushed new forms of entertainment forward but at the same time the humiliating blackface and degrading humor was really a step backwards for black life and culture. Still, black music—more specifically, black vocal music—was coming into its own. By the turn of the twentieth century, American audiences started to fall in love with the sound of barbershop music. Barbershops had become social centers where men came to jaw, jive and jam, and the sophisticated four-part

harmonies were right out of the church tradition. Years later, in the 1940s, there was a big barbershop revival that was decidedly white. Pasty white, in fact. But in its original form, barbershop music was pure black magic.

I know we're making some very broad leaps through musical history here—obviously, you could walk into any bookstore and find volumes on gospel or blues or jazz. As your humble tour guide through doo wop history, I think it's really important to understand that every player in our musical history has helped us get where we are today. Groups we mention here and the zillions of groups we don't, from the 1600s through the 1900s—every one of them has changed the course and contributed to our musical tradition.

Both doo wop and rock 'n' roll were stoked in the fires of the black experience.

This music we love is rooted in African culture and, through a long and painful process, became uniquely and identifiably our own. By the early 1900s, an incredible combination of ingredients were being mixed together in this great experiment called America. White was mixed in with black, religion with labor, south with north, agriculture with industry. America was—and is—an experiment in fusion. Music is the light and energy that poured out when those influences fused.

Nowhere is the culmination of influences so apparent as in the blues. In it we hear the propulsive rhythms of the birthplace, the sun-seared folk of the south and the lonely prayer of a wandering soul. We hear the spirituals, the field hollers and the church hymns. It's as if the entire black experience is summed up and spit out in a great blues song. In fact, if you listen for it, the raw human experience we all share is laid bare. The man on the street may not be able to express it as beautifully and may not even share the same hard history, but a true blues resonates with whatever pain is in us. Through the bluesman's struggle, the singing of his song, we get some peace. That's why the influence of the blues over the past century has been so potent. And that's why it's a fundamental part of every song that's worth a damn.

Thanks for letting Professor Brucie stand up here at the podium for a few minutes. Now I'm changing from my tweed jacket back to my leather, flipping up my shirt collar, and putting on my shades. The Mills Brothers are standing by in the next chapter and, let me tell you, you don't want to keep those guys waiting.

[1] Kebede, Ashenafi. *Roots of Black Music: The Vocal, Instrumental & Dance Heritage of Africa & Black America* . Africa World Press, 1995.

[2] Kebede, Ashenafi. *Roots of Black Music: The Vocal, Instrumental & Dance Heritage of Africa & Black America* . Africa World Press, 1995.

[3] Floyd Jr. *The Power of Black Music: Interpreting Its History from Africa to the United States.* Oxford University Press, 1996.

THE INK SPOTS

ELLA FITZGERALD

LOUIS ARMSTRONG

THE MILLS BROTHERS

The Doo Wop Pioneers

Looking back over time, one can view the history of music as a series of very broad strokes. In terms of Western music, baroque dominated in the seventeenth century, classical in the eighteenth century and romantic in the nineteenth century.

In the past one hundred years our nation has grown up in the age of vocal music. From cotton fields to churches to concert halls, the focal point of our music has been someone singing his or her heart out. The fact that it's vocal music also means it's very personal. It's about the *I*, the individual's experience, just like that caveman reporting victories to his friends. You can see it everywhere along the twentieth-century timeline. It's never distant or formal—there's no royal *We* in the blues, in early pop or in rock 'n'

roll. I think it's this intimate aspect to vocal music that has always been attractive. Our music is by the people, for the people.

Once you can identify this link—that vocal music is personal, and personal music is popular—you can start to connect the dots from blues to small-group harmonies to R&B, and eventually to doo wop.

Jazzamatazz

As bluesmen traveled our country's dusty roads, their pure style started taking on the influence of other regional sounds. New Orleans took the grit of the blues under its shell and turned out the pearl we came to know as jazz. Like America itself, jazz was characterized by a melding of diverse cultures: the style drew on European

New Orleans took the grit of the blues under its shell and turned out the pearl we came to know as jazz.

chord structures, African beats and Creole heat. Jazz also reflected the American experience in its improvisation. There was a desire in the music, as there was countrywide, to develop ideas that couldn't be found on the written page. In jazz, a great creative egg was hatched.

Jazz music provided the soundtrack for some very dark periods in our history, notably the Great Depression. It seems strange at first, but at the same time the economy was spiraling down the drain and the threat of war loomed in Europe, we were embracing jazz with its untamed celebrations and boundless energy. Maybe it was a national reaction to human tragedy like a New Orleans funeral is a response to death, where we celebrate life with every expressive shout and dance we can muster rather than wallow in self-pity and silence.

But that's what we do. We use music as shelter, to help us feel comfortable and safe. The phenomenon of bright music in dark days was mirrored a decade later, in the early 1940s, when American soldiers were at war while here at home we were in the full throes of swing jazz. To this day,

some jazz can be challenging music to hear because it is so individual and unbound by convention. But the swing bands of the thirties and forties played happy, universally enjoyable music that gave people a reason to dance in a ballroom full of friends they hadn't met yet. Even the ballads were gently swaying odes to our brothers overseas, reminding them that their gals and their families were eagerly awaiting their return. It was a great unifier at a time when sticking together was the best chance we had to survive.

The mega-stars of the swing and big band eras were also instrumental in breaking down the color barrier. White America already loved black music but, regrettably, not the black people who gave of their musical gifts. Before Louis Armstrong, whose blaring and beautiful sound trumpeted the arrival of jazz in the mainstream, it was unthinkable that a black man could be a "star." In the eras of swing and big band, we saw a litany of enormously talented people who became recognizable personalities: Billy Eckstine, Count Basie, Josephine Baker, Billie Holiday, Earl Hines, Ella Fitzgerald, Lena

BILLIE HOLIDAY

SWINGING INTO THE DOO WOP ERA

LENA HORNE

LOUIS ARMSTRONG

Jazz music is closely associated with improvisation, and there are hundreds of transcendent moments on jazz records where performers can be heard expressing themselves in beautiful, colorful solos. For artists of the swing-jazz era, which peaked in the early and mid 1940s, the chance to release their innermost voice was usually limited to solos and lead vocal lines. But these splashes of originality and self-expression had an influence on the young vocalists who would soon be singing doo wop. Jazz forged a transition that made doo wop possible, and in many ways doo wop can even be seen as the legacy of swing jazz.

While there was always a generous ebb and flow in big-band arrangements, they were still arrangements; that is, the musicians were following notes on a page, playing strict parts that contributed to the ensemble's sound at large. But against a backdrop of plush horns, a lead vocalist would sparkle and shine in the spotlight. Legends like Billie Holiday and Ella Fitzgerald played liberally against the timing and harmony of the band's orchestration, and their unpredictable improvisations on a melody would carry listeners up and away. The characteristic of an attention-grabbing lead vocal out in front of a set arrangement is fundamental to doo wop as well. Think of Billy Eckstine's romantic vibrato on "Stormy Monday Blues" with Earl Hines' orchestra humming in the background; now recall Tony Williams belting out "The Great Pretender" supported by the Platters' watercolor wash of vocals behind him. The quartets and quintets of doo wop were like big bands in condensed form.

SARAH VAUGHAN

BILLY ECKSTINE

FRANK SINATRA

Of course, no self-respecting doo wopper would deny that the genre got its start when singers sought to imitate band instruments with their voices. It was an efficient—not to mention economical—way to recreate the sounds of a band, and throughout the history of doo wop you can hear vocalists sounding like string basses, trombones and raspy saxophones. Even the nasally sound of a cup-muted trumpet could be imitated by an adept vocalist singing into the hollow of his hands. The Mills Brothers, founding fathers of doo wop, were famous for fooling audiences into thinking they were playing horns and strings.

Another staple of doo wop was the singing of so-called "nonsense" syllables. These oddball enunciations are usually explained as another means of imitating an instrument—a quality they share with the "scat" singing identified with improvisational jazz vocalists, especially Ella Fitzgerald. Listeners seemed to love the departure from traditional lyrics, and both doo wop and jazz took the use of syllable-singing to new levels. In doo wop, it's evident everywhere from the famous yip-yip-yip/mum-mum-mum of the Silhouettes' "Get A Job" to the Cameos' chorus of "Shanga Langa Ding Dong."

Doo wop artists borrowed quite a bit from songbooks of old, too, and many of their classics had been hits for the jazz bands that came before. Just a few of the many examples include "In The Still of the Night" (Five Satins and Billy Eckstine), "Blue Moon" (the Marcels and Glen Gray) and "Stormy Weather" (the Spaniels and Lena Horne).

The Ames Brothers

Like most siblings, each of the Ames had professional aspirations separate and apart from his brothers. Only Joe, the eldest, wanted to study opera singing, while brothers Gene, Vic and Ed were interested in sports or acting. But their mother had spent the 1920s giving birth to boys, and if she wanted them to sing, well, sing they would.

The boys were from Malden, Massachusetts, and were actually born under the name Urick. In the early days they had borrowed Vic's middle name and called themselves the Amory Brothers, eventually adopting the Ames name after signing to Coral Records in 1948. Coral quickly proved they knew what worked in the record industry, and the Ames Brothers charted within a year, even before hitting it big in January of 1951 with "Rag Mop." The B-side of the same record was "Sentimental Me," making for a chart-topping twofer that put the group on a fast track to success. Major hits soon followed with "Undecided" and their biggest smash, "You You You."

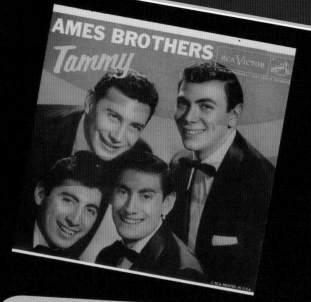

The Ames Brothers had a long and successful career, and by the time they closed up shop in 1959 they had logged more than 50 songs on the charts. Being an all-white group, they had many advantages over black singing groups, including the promise of airplay, and they played to the masses with their safe, sanitized selections. There's one title in their catalog that sounds a little risqué—"The Naughty Lady of Shady Lane"—but the song turns out to be about a nine-day-old baby! That was characteristic of the Ames Brothers, who had a sense of theatrics and were such good performers that they were regularly asked to guest on television's early variety shows. Ed Ames, the baby and best known of the bunch, went on to perform on Broadway and to star as Mingo the Indian on the *Daniel Boone* TV series of the late 1960s.

Horne—these were not just musicians but celebrities. Black celebrities.

The Small Group Goes Big Time

Young artists have always seen their way to new sights and sounds by standing on the shoulders of the giants who came before. Two vocal groups, the Mills Brothers and the Ink Spots, borrowed the sophisticated harmonies and cool-headed class of the jazz era to appeal to remarkably broad audiences. They also imitated jazz-band instruments with their voices and represented in small groups what the swing bands achieved with full-blown orchestras. Within a few years, the best doo wop groups would reach new heights by standing on the shoulders of the Mills Brothers and the Ink Spots.

When it came to putting the cornerstones of twentieth-century vocal music in place, the Mills Brothers did all the heavy lifting. These four brothers from Piqua, Ohio, intuitively understood what audiences loved in barbershop, blues, swing and pop music, and rolled it all up into one neat little package. They were masters at mimicking instruments with their voices—despite what listeners heard, early Mills recordings specified: "No musical instruments or mechanical devices used on this recording other than one guitar." Similarly, the Ink Spots were greatly influenced by jazz arrangements. Their 1939 breakthrough hit "If I Didn't Care" carried echoes of an Ellington ballad such as "In A Sentimental Mood"; the vibrato in Bill Kenny's high tenor shivered like a soprano sax, and Orville "Hoppy" Jones resonated on the low

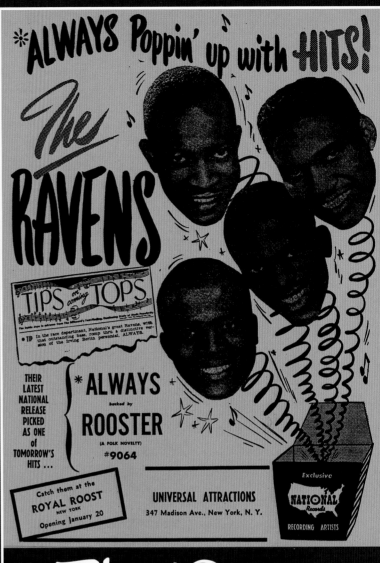

The Ravens

I f any single group represents the starting point of doo wop's evolution, it's the Ravens. They were the big bang at the start of the doo wop universe. Formed in 1945 Harlem, the group is credited with many firsts, including their ornithological name and adding pizzazz to their stage act with dance steps. But the most formative influence on the music to follow was how the Ravens turned vocal harmony on its head: rather than having the tenor man sing lead, Jimmy Ricks was out front with his booming bass. In doo wop music, as in no music before or since, it's the "low man" on the totem pole who gets all the respect.

When it came to putting the cornerstones of twentieth-century vocal music in place, the Mills Brothers did all the heavy lifting.

end like a string bass. Rich midrange voices filled the space between, and tinkling piano fills laced it all together.

Within the confines of their tight vocal quartets, the Mills Brothers and the Ink Spots managed to incorporate the orchestrations of a seventeen-piece band, the swing of a horn section, and the feel-good appeal of a barbershop melody. Before them, many black artists (be they gospel, blues, jazz or otherwise) had attracted white audiences only after building their fan base on home turf. But from the time of the Mills Brothers' first hit, "Tiger Rag," in 1931, their trendsetting brand of vocal music was dropped squarely in the mainstream.

It's significant that the success of both groups was partly due to easy assimilation. Plainly said, there was nothing challenging about a Mills Brothers or an Ink Spots song. The music may have been incredibly difficult to perform but it was extremely easy-going on the listener. These were safe songs—a key factor that would later characterize most doo wop as well. Even if the music wasn't to a listener's taste, it still never rubbed anybody the wrong way.

The Mills and the Spots were smooth as cream and sweet as apple pie, and white audiences gobbled them up. Each of them had their own radio show, appeared in movies and achieved international fame. The Mills scored 71 chart hits (71!) and the Ink Spots hit 46 times, setting both groups among the most successful acts of all time. The doo wop greats to follow would take a valuable lesson.

THE AUTOMAT PAVES THE WAY FOR THE GOLDEN ARCHES

Salisbury steak, mashed potatoes and carrots…to this day I can still taste those wonderful Automat meals instantly accessible for the price of a few nickels. The true beginning of "fast food," the Automat came to New York City in 1912 and remained popular throughout the 1950s as a purveyor of inexpensive, but nourishing, ready-to-eat meals. Some of my fondest childhood memories are those of my father bringing me to this special place, where row upon row of hot and cold dishes waited behind individual chrome-plated windows for me to drop in my coins, slowly turn the dial and then slip into my eager hands. Even better, another plate would then appear magically behind the window ready to entice the next bedazzled, hungry kid.

The suburban sprawl and the car culture that followed World War II, plus the rising cost of food, all contributed to the eventual demise of the Automat. But in 1955, another contender was ready to take its place: McDonald's. When those Golden Arches went up, they were like a stairway to heaven for a teenager. They said, "Come to me, I'll feed you." Even for a young man of limited resources, here was an opportunity to take a girl out for a meal. I don't think anybody in those days could have foreseen what McDonald's would become or where it would eventually rate on the food chain, and we didn't care. For us, it was new, it was happening and all part of making the scene.

The Andrews Sisters

Darlings of radio and sweethearts of the U.S.O., the Andrews Sisters represented more to us than light-hearted hits like "Shoo-Shoo Baby" and "Don't Sit Under the Apple Tree" ever hinted. Few groups before or since have been so woven into our national conscience. Listening to one of their songs today provides more than a nostalgic reverie—it invokes images of a nation at war, of a looming threat in Europe and the boys we sent to keep it at bay.

A very rare mix of talent and timing is responsible for the Andrews' role in America's history. Heavily influenced by the Boswell Sisters, another trio of siblings singing in close harmony, the girls came to national attention late in the 1930s. The voices of LaVerne, Maxene and Patty were nearly indistinguishable from one another, and their harmonies melded together as if they were a single singer with three sets of vocal chords. Though they really looked quite different from one another, to this day we picture them as a matched set, all in Army outfits and offering a smiley salute. As America entered the mid-1940s, one of its darkest times, we clung to the warmth and wholesome charm of the Andrews girls.

During World War II, the Andrews Sisters were a source of comfort for the men stationed abroad and for the families who awaited their safe return. They flirted with the "Boogie Woogie Bugle Boy" from Company B, and cheered for victory in "Hot Time in the Town of Berlin." Bing Crosby often joined the girls in sending a message of hope to stateside families and friends, perhaps most famously on "Ac-Cent-Tchu-Ate the Positive." Even if you were stuck in a snowy trench somewhere near the Belgian border, hearing the Andrews Sisters come over the airwaves was a sure sign that, far across the ocean, someone was leaving a light on back home.

DR. BENJAMIN SPOCK'S CHILD CARE REVOLUTION

When Dr. Spock published *Baby and Child Care* in 1946, it turned traditional child rearing on its ear, or rear! Parents who were warned that sparing the rod would spoil the child now had a pediatrician advocating more love, understanding and less rigidity with their infants. He was later accused of helping sow the permissive seeds of the first generation to come of age under his influence, the hippies and flower children of the 1960s. He denied this, stating that he advocated mutual respect between parents and children—not a bad philosophy for any age. He also wasn't afraid to buck the establishment by protesting against the Vietnam War and warning against the potential hazards of nuclear energy.

The Record Biz Gets Busy

The mass appeal of black music was not lost on the record business. Their antennae had been up for years; way back in 1917, the Original Dixieland Jass Band had sold over one million records. Dozens of labels later came calling, including notables such as King, Jubilee, Savoy, Red Robin, Old Town, Alladin, Chess and Federal. They realized there was a tremendous market to capitalize on, but also that there was talent deserving of exposure. Populating the labels were businessmen, many of them guys from New York and Philadelphia, who had a genuine affinity for black music and culture.

Somewhere along the line, record companies got a bad name. They became the enemy, the "suits" who wanted to turn art into commodity. Now, in many cases that reputation has been well earned. Plus, no one has ever started a business to lose money. But many of these early labels really had their heart in it, and in truth they deserve a lot of credit. No one is saying a black artist never got a raw deal—in fact, most of them did, and doo wop history is scarred by their stories. However, many so-called suits had courage to get behind this music when there was a great deal of racism and hatred in the air. Labels would pay for releases to be recorded, printed and distributed just to see them shoved into the back bins of music stores and labeled "race music." What a disgrace that was. Even with the huge obstacle of racism, though, these labels would release 15 or 20 records by an artist whether they had charted or not. Fans of vocal music—fans of any music today, really—owe a debt to several of those early labels.

THE ORIOLES

The Orioles can be likened to the Ravens' crosstown rivals. Though their influence on musicians to follow may not have been quite as strong, they were more productive in the studio and unrivaled in pulling audiences. Named for their home state's bird (just like the baseball team), Baltimore's Orioles were formed by lead tenor Sonny Til.

UNCLE MILTIE AND THE GOLDEN AGE OF TELEVISION

By 1948, some strange, aluminum branches had begun sprouting from American rooftops. Neighbors eyed them with envy. Inside, families and friends sat transfixed by a magic box—a "radio with pictures."

Early television looked pretty primitive, by today's standards. Coarse black and white images were transmitted to tiny "direct-view" screens, and broadcasters couldn't fill more than about four hours of content each evening. Even in its nascent state, though, television was a cultural watershed. Viewers were amazed to watch live images sent from somewhere across town, or even from another city. We were awed by television right from the start, and owning a television quickly became a symbol of status and sophistication. The bigger the better, too, and a family with a 12-inch screen would be dethroned when the neighbors bought a 15" x 20" projection screen. Within a matter of months, a city block with a few aluminum branches grew into a forest of antennas.

When television first gained popularity, we'd watch anything. People held television parties, and if there was nothing else on, the partygoers would sit there in front of a test pattern! Early broadcasts of boxing matches or kids' serials like *Captain Video and His Video Rangers* drew the attention of anyone who owned a TV, but the first golden age of television dawned when *Texaco Star Theater* began its run in 1948.

Sponsored by the Texaco Oil Company, the show had its roots in a long-running radio show of the same name. Even before audiences glimpsed the elastic face of host Milton Berle, he had won their hearts over the radiowaves with his comedy. Berle was ideally positioned to become the first TV star, and he earned the nickname "Mr. Television" not only because of his celebrity but because he personally was responsible for selling more televisions than Montgomery Ward could keep in stock. "Uncle Miltie," as we came to know him, was a vaudeville-styled comic who could be childish, naughty, silly or heart-warming. He was all things to all audiences, and he brought families together in front of the glowing tube.

In the age of *Texaco Star Theater*, Tuesday nights were sacrosanct. Restaurants would close and movies played to empty theaters while families gathered to share an hour with Uncle Miltie. He'd do anything for a laugh: walk like a zombie, dress up as Cleopatra, perform magic tricks, sing an off-key tune. *Star Theater* was a variety show, too, and set the stage for shows hosted by the likes of Jack Benny and Fred Allen. For the duration of the show's run, Uncle Miltie was inextricably linked to our nation's blossoming love affair with television. Those of us who grew up with Berle's charm warming our home living room still hear his voice every time we reach for the remote at the end of the night. "Listen to your Uncle Miltie," he'd say, "and go to bed."

Soul Stirrers

What a name! This group lives up to its own billing, too. The Soul Stirrers get footnoted in vocal music history because a famous singer came through their ranks, but there was much more to this Houston, Texas, outfit than a training ground.

Long before the term "soul" was used to describe the core of rhythm and blues music, the Soul Stirrers were reaching listeners deep down inside. They quite simply revolutionized gospel music. The Soul Stirrers somehow managed to take transcendent, spiritual elements that had been the domain of rural church music and recast them in passionate songs for a secular audience. They also

overturned convention by featuring two lead singers, so the supporting voices never lost any power when dual leads stepped out front. When the group needed a new second lead to fill an empty slot late in 1950, a 19-year-old from Chicago answered the call. The sweet, romantic voice of the young Sam Cooke was the perfect counterpart to Hall Foster's traditional "shout" style, and helped the group expand their audience far beyond the back pew.

No group outside the church had tapped the sacred well before, and the ripples of the Soul Stirrers' influence can be heard in all the soulful music to follow, from Aretha Franklin to Gladys Knight to Little Richard.

Squeaky Clean and Peachy Keen

The music played on as America, in 1941, entered World War II—one of the most monumental conflicts ever to shape mankind. In times of conflict, it's human nature for people to stay close to home and not stray from the familiar. We huddle, and in these times we are unwelcoming to jarring changes in culture. It was in this atmosphere that a featureless and whitewashed pop music emerged and then thrived for ten years. There was a vague connection to the singers who had fronted big bands in the years prior, but in this bland context performers like Vic Damone, Bing Crosby, Dinah Shore, Doris Day, Vaughn Monroe and the like rarely showed much soul or imagination.

There were a few bright spots. Some pop artists showed real ingenuity and had the good taste to share composers and arrangers with the more soulful jazz and vocal groups. The Andrews Sisters were the finest example. There must be something to harmonizing with people who share the same gene pool: though none of them could read music, the girls fell seamlessly into their neatly trimmed three-part harmonies. LaVerne, Maxene and Patty, inspired by the Boswell Sisters before them, were a big hit stateside and a thrill to the eyes and ears of GI's stationed overseas. Songs for soldiers like "Don't Sit Under the Apple Tree" and "Boogie Woogie Bugle Boy" warmed the airwaves of Armed Forces Radio, while "Ac-Cent-Tchu-Ate the Positive" kept the lights on at home.

JOE McCARTHY AND THE RED SCARE

The euphoria felt at the end of World War II soon gave way to a new kind of war—cold and murky, where for a brief period starting in 1950, a zealot named Joseph McCarthy held America hostage. The first time I really focused on the Senator from Wisconsin's accusations and agenda, it changed my life and my attitude about politics. Letting someone like McCarthy garner enough power to feed the fires of paranoia, then use a Senate committee to abuse countless Americans under the guise of rooting out the new enemy, communists, was very wrong. Many careers and lives were ruined before he was finally stopped in 1954. His turbulent rise and fall was a wake-up call for America. It taught us to get involved and stay involved. People always say it can't happen again, but it can. We should never forget.

For a boy growing up in Brooklyn, New York, Ebbets Field—home of the Brooklyn Dodgers—was a magical place. While I knew that a baseball game was a fantastic spectacle, I had no concept that what went on inside those walls could affect the way people think. But Jackie Robinson changed our world for the better.

Jack Roosevelt Robinson was born in Georgia and grew up in California. At UCLA, his incredible athleticism earned him a national reputation for excellence in football, basketball, track and baseball. His talent as a professional baseball player was initially relegated to the American Negro Leagues, where he played for the Kansas City Royals until 1945. That was the year he signed on with the Dodgers. After a banner year on their farm team, he became the first black player of the twentieth century to play in the major leagues.

Even as he led his team to one win after the other, Robinson sustained a regular assault of dehumanizing bigotry from fans and players alike. His own teammates signed a petition to keep him off the club, and the same people who cheered his team from the bleachers sent him death threats. Pitchers aimed fast balls at his head and basemen dug their spikes into his legs. But Jackie stood strong, tall and steady. He won Rookie of the Year in 1947, MVP in 1949, and helped the Dodgers win the 1955 World Series against their crosstown rivals, the New York Yankees.

Of course, Jackie Robinson's victories resonated far beyond the four corners of a baseball diamond. He helped teach a lesson that every school kid knows today: that talent and determination can prevail over ignorance and stupidity. Long after his baseball career ended, Robinson continued to lead by example, influencing the likes of President John F. Kennedy, Dr. Martin Luther King and Nelson D. Rockefeller. The civil rights movement and ethnic integration would still be profound hurdles for black Americans; to this day, our nation could learn a lesson or two from the ballfield. But Robinson hit a home run for African Americans, and his success marks one of our country's proudest moments. His number, 42, is long retired now, but Jackie Robinson is a champion for all time.

Jackie Robinson Breaks the Major League Color Barrier

JACKIE ROBINSON IN THE JACKIE ROBINSON STORY

Once the nightmare of World War II was behind us, people across the United States turned their hopes once again to the American dream. A comfortable home, a pretty neighborhood, maybe a swing under the apple tree…was this too much to ask? Though the desires of the masses were modest, there was a housing crunch in the late '40s, due in no small part to the thousands of GI's who returned from the war wanting to build new homes for their young families.

Enter developer Levitt & Sons with a plan that would forever change the picture of America's middle class. William J. Levitt (one of the sons) sought to build affordable housing in a desirable area, and bought up land on Long Island, New York, that had been used for potato farming. Here, halfway between New York City and the growing industrial areas further out on the island, beginning in 1947 Levitt constructed more than 17,000 single-family homes. The models were manufactured at an incredible pace and sold at an incredible price: under $8,000, making for monthly payments on a Levitt "ranch" less than $60. Soon the potato fields were a kaleidoscope of little houses.

Levitt was not just selling houses; he was building communities. There were sprawling common spaces for kids to play and dogs to run; there were Levittown post offices and grocery stores and gas stations. Neighbors played cards together, watched their kids together and waved each other across the backyard to come have a martini. The concept was so successful that a second Levittown was started in Pennsylvania in 1952, and similar neighborhoods would eventually be built all across the country for decades to come. Levittown was more than affordable housing—high-rises and housing projects already existed in the inner cities. William J. and company poured the concrete of modern suburbia.

The name "Levittown" is often used critically to imply conformity, as if we've all been sold on the idea of wanting the same kitchen, the same car, the same life. But in the postwar era, it was an easy entry into the middle class. For tens of thousands of families, Levittown represented the chance to have a slice of American pie.

Levittown

The Delta River Boys

Delta River Boys may not be a familiar name, but the sheer volume of their output and the longevity of their career has secured their place in vocal history. Hailing from Oklahoma, they launched a career that spanned fifty years—easier, admittedly, with an ever-changing lineup, but still a rarity in the world of music. They had only one hit that made the charts: "Just A-Sittin and A-Rockin'" reached #17 in 1945. At that time, just three years into their career, the Boys had already released twenty-three sides. Even with this lone run up the charts, they were reliable hit-makers and popular performers. In fact, their ongoing claim to fame—aside from using up a few tons of record shellac—is that they performed in more movies than any other singing group, including the Beatles. By 1956, the Delta River Boys had been seen in fifteen films.

The Andrews Sisters may have been an easy sell at the time, but that's what the country needed. They also helped keep the bar high for vocal music while bringing down the barriers for latter-day doo wop singers who would face the dual challenge of being black and female.

More than any decade prior, vocal music came into its own in the 1940s. Amid the success of Mills Brothers, the Ink Spots and the Andrews Sisters, outfits like the Delta Rhythm Boys, Four Vagabonds, Five Red Caps and the Four Knights were heard loud and clear en route to the doo wop destination.

Enter the Blackbirds

If the Mills Brothers poured the foundation of doo wop music, the Ravens put up the first, second and third floors. They built to a height that provided a view to doo wop's future.

In 1946, it was the Ravens who first combined the definitive elements of doo wop style in the song "Lullabye." The vocal arrangements were divided into distinct parts, with a high tenor soaring over the top, midrange harmonies painting a palette of ooh and ahh, and a thick, punchy bass. It was the bass part, especially, that set the Ravens apart. At the bottom end of this seminal doo wop sound were percussive syllables that mimicked the attack of string basses and cellos, delivered by a rich, deep voice that was distinctly black.

Even more so than the Ink Spots before them, the Ravens were notable for owning their ethnicity. Certainly jazz had broken down the

The Mills Brothers

Every music group to have sung vocal harmony in the past seventy-five years owes a debt to Herbert, Donald, Harry, and John Mills, Jr. Performing as teenagers in the 1920s, the quartet's original routine was to imitate instruments on the kazoo. One night they accidentally left their kazoos at home and quickly covered by mimicking band instruments with their voices alone, and by cupping their hands over their mouths to imitate muted horns. Audiences were amazed. The Mills Brothers' novelty act soon blossomed into a highly regarded career that endured for over forty years.

Vocal music came into its own in the 1940s...the Delta Rhythm Boys, Four Vagabonds, Five Red Caps and the Four Knights were en route to the doo wop destination.

color line, with black artists drawing an ever-growing white audience, but the most successful artists had done so by becoming more white. Take a look at the photos of those earlier stars. It's almost as if a trick of photography made them appear Caucasian—if not in their softened skin tones, then in the way they wore their hair and neatly tailored suits. The raven is a black bird. Like the Ink Spots before them, they didn't hide their blackness. Rather, they wore it on their sleeve.

The Orioles—another ensemble of black birds—were the counterpart to the Ravens, and broke in 1948 with "It's Too Soon To Know." Whereas the Ravens made their mark with up-tempo jump tunes, the Orioles were known for their ballads and liquid lines. They too laid a strong foundation with a bass vocalist and set soothing alto breaths across the middle while a falsetto tenor cut a high line across the top. In hits like "Tell Me So" and "I Cover the Waterfront," one can detect not only doo wop DNA but a genetic link to rhythm & blues. Romantic ballads later became a mainstay of the doo wop genre, and nobody could pull the heartstrings like the Orioles.

The style, talent and black pride of the Ravens and the Orioles were contagious. Audiences returned time and time again to their sweet sounds, resulting in a stream of hits for both groups that lasted well into the '50s. And following in their flight pattern came the first flock of doo wop musicians. Doo wop's day had dawned, and the birds were singing.

THE INK SPOTS

At the core of the Ink Spots' sound is an identifiably ethnic intonation, most notably in the famous talking bass parts of Orville "Hoppy" Jones. Considering that the Ink Spots came to fame in the late 1930s, their success in gaining the widespread appreciation of white audiences while holding tightly to their identity is remarkable. Remember that in 1935, when the Ink Spots first became known, the civil rights movement was still two decades down the road. The name, Ink Spots, has the ring of discrimination today. But perhaps it was intended to be self-effacing; when tenor man Deek Watson broke off to start his own group, he named them the Brown Dots.

The Larks

"My Reverie," the group's breakthrough recording, is so plush and tantalizing that it's hard to imagine anyone not falling in love with the Larks. With velvety tones as rich as a string orchestra's, the range and depth of their talent is on full display. They are accompanied only by piano, though it's hard, on first listen, to believe that the bass line is sung and not played on an upright. Far above, Gene Mumford's airy lead tenor floats like a haunted angel.

Mumford was indeed haunted, having served two years' prison time on a North Carolina chain gang before the governor confirmed his alibi and gave him a full pardon. He had been invited to join the Larks just before the wrongful accusation and, thankfully, the boys welcomed his return.

Melancholy tunes were the group's strong suit though they could just as handily stir up a rousing jump rhythm, as on "Coffee, Cigarettes and Tears" and the rockin' "Little Sidecar." The original Larks line-up lasted only two years, but in that time they released eleven singles that grace the collections of doo wop's most discriminating connoisseurs.

THE DOMINOES

CHAPTER 3
1951–1954

The Music Grows Up

Great musicians and artists have one foot in the future. Their vision offers a sneak peek at what's around the next bend. But music does not set the stage for our lives; rather, the world sets the stage for music.

The early 1950s were a pivotal time for our nation politically, socially and artistically. With World War II behind us and the economy on an upswing, we had the makings of a stable nation, but the ground was shifting beneath us. The war had somehow increased the scale of everything: our potential to do good things was greater, our power was mightier—and our problems were exponentially bigger, too.

In the deserts of Nevada we tested atomic bombs that had "the power of the sun." Fearing that the new war in Korea could grow into a third World War, President Truman pulled General MacArthur out of Asia. Worse yet, we were becoming divided right here on our home turf due to the "Red Scare." It was a dark moment in our history—though sadly not an isolated one—when Ethel and Julius Rosenberg were put to death for treason. To this day, their family continues to seek some form of restitution. We lost a lot when we lost our trust in one another.

With our brave new world undercut by paranoia and uncertainty, one might expect the music of the early fifties to have been dark and foreboding, maybe even atonal (and on the classical front, much of it was). So why was pop music so polite and neat, with its shirt tucked in and every hair in place? Because in times of uncertainty, we seek

ANNETTE FUNICELLO

Early Children's Television

Before children's television became an electronic babysitter, it was not unusual for parents to gather around the TV set with their kids. Early shows like *Kukla, Fran and Ollie*, presented material for all ages. A lively puppet show with one human character, Fran Allison, carrying on a running dialogue with her spirited co-stars, *Kukla, Fran and Ollie* enjoyed a ten-year run from 1947 to 1957.

Though *Kukla, Fran and Ollie* had a loyal fan base, *Howdy Doody* (1947-1960) became a baby boomer smash. Originally called *The Puppet Playhouse*, it was set in the fictional town of Doodyville and filmed in front of a live audience of children sitting in the famous "peanut gallery." The show cleverly mixed puppets like the affable Howdy Doody, Mr. Bluster and Princess SummerFallWinterSpring with live actors, including host Buffalo Bob Smith and the mute Clarabell the Clown. Clarabell later brought a nationwide audience to tears by speaking two words at the end of the last show: "Goodbye, Kids."

Meanwhile, the world's most famous mouse and his plucky band of Mouseketeers was teaching America to sing "M – I – C – K – E – Y M – O – U – S – E." Produced by the Walt Disney entertainment machine, *The Mickey Mouse Club* (1955-1959) featured a kid-themed variety show which aired five days a week. Annette Funicello was the show's breakout Mouseketeer, with children across America watching her every move. The Mouseketeers eventually succumbed to changing tastes, but *The Mickey Mouse Club* played a critical role in shaping children's television.

The show cleverly mixed puppets like the affable Howdy Doody, Mr. Bluster and Princess SummerFall Winter-Spring with live actors, including host Buffalo Bob Smith and the mute Clarabell the Clown.

Billy Ward and His Dominoes

Few doo wop groups managed to hold on to all their original members, but none could boast a string of lead singers like those who fronted the Dominoes (also known as Billy Ward and His Dominoes).

The very first incarnation of the band included Clyde McPhatter, who quickly led them up the charts in 1950 with "Do Something for Me" before the legendary "Sixty Minute Man" was released in 1951. "Sixty Minute Man" was no fluke, either; it stayed at #1 all that summer and was followed with hits like "Have Mercy Baby" and "The Bells" before McPhatter left in 1953, the same year he formed The Drifters.

The Dominoes would have probably been doomed were it not for the addition of a fast-talking boxer with a high tenor strong enough to go the rounds. And that voice be-longed to nineteen-year-old Jackie Wilson. Fans who were ready to give up on the Dominoes couldn't believe the group had come up with McPhatter's equal, and with barely a pause the group was back up in the stratosphere of the pop and R&B charts. When Wilson left in 1957 to pursue his solo career, Eugene Mumford—former leader of the Larks and the Serenaders—amply filled the lead spot.

So who was Billy Ward? He was an accomplished composer and arranger, formally trained at the Juilliard School of Music in New York. In putting together his first group, Ward gathered a quartet of former vocal students and accompanied them on piano. The group was first formed as the Ques—with Clyde McPhatter billed as Clyde Ward to feign that he and Billy were brothers.

Why was pop music so polite and neat, with its shirt tucked in and every hair in place?

comfort and familiarity. The whole house was shaking and people needed a steady post to hold on to. So radio threw softballs like Bing Crosby, Doris Day, Debbie Reynolds and Perry Como. You can see the same safe-and-sound trend all over entertainment and pop culture of the time, from the movie *Show Boat* to the Broadway musical *Peter Pan*. The enduring images churned out by the entertainment industry in the early fifties spoke to our need for security and comfort. You might even call it escapism—or denial.

Vocal music played along, too, though everything that would come to define doo wop was falling into place. This, after all, was the dawn of doo wop (though it wouldn't be known by that name for years to come). I like to think of this time, starting in 1951, as the intersection of "the three T's": Talent, Trade and Technology.

Talent

The talent emerging between the years 1951 and 1954 was undeniable. The Mills Brothers, Ink Spots, Ravens and Orioles had played a de facto role as teachers, and their graduating class was full of star pupils. In the early fifties, the careers of the Flamingos, the Moonglows and the Harptones were all launched. Clyde McPhatter led the Dominoes and the Drifters, and Lee Andrews led the Hearts. The Crows crowed and the Clovers got lucky! This new generation not only secured the success of doo wop to follow, but set the bar high for a genre that was characterized by quality and class.

Gathered in small groups—almost always a quartet or quintet—the young vocal harmonists began to establish a set of loose guidelines for their music. Prior vocal groups often featured full-group

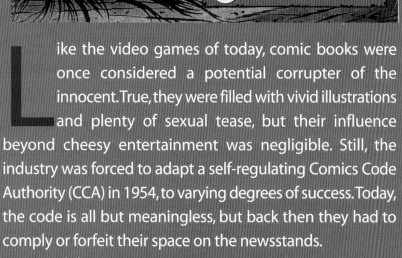

Like the video games of today, comic books were once considered a potential corrupter of the innocent. True, they were filled with vivid illustrations and plenty of sexual tease, but their influence beyond cheesy entertainment was negligible. Still, the industry was forced to adapt a self-regulating Comics Code Authority (CCA) in 1954, to varying degrees of success. Today, the code is all but meaningless, but back then they had to comply or forfeit their space on the newsstands.

Meanwhile, in 1955 an irreverent comic book called *Mad* became *Mad* magazine, over which the CCA had no jurisdiction. Filled with gleeful swipes at politicians, authority figures and anything mainstream, *Mad* and mascot Alfred E. Neuman kept us thinking in an era of Cold War paranoia.

On the other end of the spectrum, cartoonist Charles M. Schulz created his classic Sunday comic strip *Peanuts* in 1950. His multifaceted cast of cartoon children were wise beyond their ages, each drawing on life's daily highs and lows to comment on our society. Schulz retired from the strip in 1999 and died shortly afterward, but Charlie Brown, his dog Snoopy and the Peanuts gang had long since become a beloved part of our popular culture.

MAD

No. 30   DEC .56

Write-in Candidate for President
ALFRED E. NEUMAN
says
"WHAT—ME WORRY?"

Doo wop just ain't doo wop without a bottom-feeding bassline.

harmonies, but now each vocalist followed a distinct line. Whereas the lead vocals in earlier groups sang in a high tenor, more leaders now sang in falsetto. Nolan Strong of the Diablos was probably the premier falsetto singer in doo wop; he raised the style to such a height that Smokey Robinson considered him a hero.

Unlike the airy sound of a tenor, falsetto singing cuts off any air flow to the nose, producing a thinner, reedy sound that sometimes takes on a nasal quality. It also sends the singer's range flying up above tenor into the alto range—leaving a wide midrange open for the other vocalists to fill. Second tenors and baritones would wash the space with breathy *doo-wah* type sounds, sometimes called "blow harmonies." More than any other group, the Moonglows patented the blow-harmony sound with their warm, deep middle voices (check out early hits like "Most of All" and "When I'm With You") and influenced countless groups to follow.

On the bottom end, bass singers honored the "low as you can go" tradition. But their vocal attacks now became more percussive; rather than offering languid lines held out for several measures at a time, they sounded like string basses being smacked with the wrong side of a bow. No longer just part of the scenery, the bass man had his own active pattern to follow throughout a tune. Try and imagine any of the old hits without a contagious, bottom-feeding bass line—doo wop just ain't doo wop without it.

In fact, there's a great tune by Johnny Cymbal called "Mr. Bass Man," in which Johnny sings the part

THE SPANIELS

Being from Gary, Indiana, the Spaniels were a rare offering from the midwest. Other than that geographic irregularity, their career closely follows the boilerplate of doo wop.

The quartet formed in high school and got their start at a talent show. They must have had a healthy sense of humor, having decided on their name after the bass player's girlfriend said they sounded like a bunch of dogs. But they howled in harmony well enough to convince the owners of a local record shop to start a label on their behalf. Vee-Jay Records would in time move to Chicago, where it became a cornerstone of rhythm and blues. (History also marks Vee-Jay for being the first American label to release songs by the Beatles.)

In grand doo wop tradition, the Spaniels' turn under the spotlight was brief though bright. "Baby, It's You" was a jukebox favorite in 1953, and in 1954 they hit with "Goodnight, Sweetheart, Goodnight," which was noted for a great saxophone imitation by bass singer Gerald Gregory. But the Spaniels' own version of "Goodnight" was soon overshadowed when white singers, the McGuire Sisters, sent their cover of it to #7.

That wasn't the only time fame and fortune would slip from their paws. According to rock 'n' roll legend, in 1958 a gospel group called the Nightingales offered the Spaniels a Hank Ballard-penned song entitled "The Twist." The Nightingales feared they would lose their gospel base if they recorded a secular song, and offered it to the Spaniels—who passed. Chubby Checker did not make the same mistake.

Classic Television Comedies and Sitcoms

THE NELSON FAMILY

Simple, escapist entertainment dominated television throughout much of the 1950s, which was just what we wanted after World War II and the Korean War. Out of this electronic fantasy world, timeless classics such as *I Love Lucy* and *The Honeymooners* emerged. Whether it was to watch the peerless Lucille Ball as Lucy Ricardo hawking Vitameatavegamin, or Jackie Gleason's endearing everyman Ralph Kramden mired in his latest fiasco, viewers tuned in each week to share their hare-brained schemes. We all knew that by the end of each episode, Lucy and Ralph would somehow survive intact because that was the message of the time—everything will work out in the end.

It was also the era of the homogenized and pasteurized family unit, on situation-comedy precursors such as the Cleavers of *Leave it to Beaver* and the real-life Nelson clan of *Ozzie and Harriet*. Family roles were clearly defined in these small-screen enclaves; loving moms ran the household, girls and boys did not get into any serious trouble, and fathers really did know best. Nonsense, of course, but viewers happily embraced the fantasy for a few hours.

Television in the 1950s did pioneer serious dramas and edgy morality plays, on groundbreaking shows like *Playhouse 90* and *The Twilight Zone*, but for its signature comedies and sitcoms, problems faded on fadeout, and all was right with the world.

VITAMEATAVEGAMIN
FOR HEALTH

LUCILLE BALL (AS LUCY RICARDO)

JACKIE GLEASON (AS RALPH KRAMDEN), ART CARNEY (AS ED NORTON), AUDREY MEADOWS (AS ALICE KRAMDEN), JOYCE RANDOLPH (AS TRIXIE NORTON)

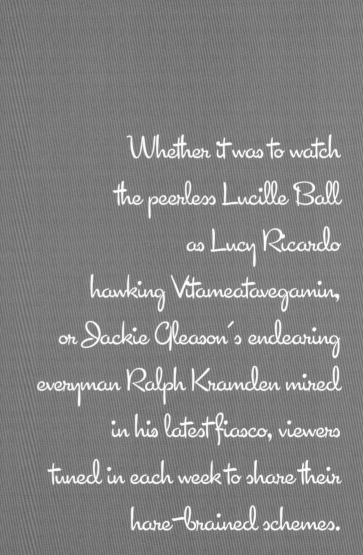

Whether it was to watch the peerless Lucille Ball as Lucy Ricardo hawking Vitameatavegamin, or Jackie Gleason's endearing everyman Ralph Kramden mired in his latest fiasco, viewers tuned in each week to share their hare-brained schemes.

FULL *dynamics-frequency* SPECTRUM ATLANTIC 8041

THE DRIFTERS' GREATEST HITS

The Drifters

The Drifters' genealogy is probably the most complex of all the doo wop groups. Their name is fitting since the talent drifted in from so many places. But they just as frequently drifted apart.

The Drifters first gelled when Ahmet Ertegun, the music-industry legend who co-founded Atlantic Records, fell in love with the voice of Clyde McPhatter. McPhatter was an early R&B singer who had been the frontman for the Dominoes, and he had a gospel-tinged tenor that was just phenomenal. Ertegun signed McPhatter in 1953 and let him put together his own supporting group. Before the first song was even recorded, a dozen members had passed through the ranks of the Drifters. But by the end of the year they had a #1 hit with "Money Honey," and they would string together hit after hit for the next fifteen years to come.

McPhatter's soaring voice defined the sweet sound of the Drifters throughout the band's lifetime, which is pretty amazing when you consider that he left just one year later. When he headed off to pursue a solo career in 1954, he sold his interest in the group to his manager, George Treadwell. That's when the Drifters really became more a business than a band. Treadwell (who was behind the success of his first wife, jazz great Sarah Vaughan) was certainly a man who knew how to make a hit song, but it seems he could never hold on to a band. And unless they were producing hits, perhaps he didn't want to.

A monumental shift in the Drifters lineup came at Treadwell's hand one night at the legendary Apollo Theater in Harlem. It was May 30, 1958, and the Drifters hadn't had a big hit in over a year. Another band on the bill that night was the Crowns, who had enjoyed just a taste of regional success, and Treadwell liked what he heard. According to rock 'n' roll legend, Treadwell simply fired the Drifters on the spot and bought the Crowns. Right there, backstage at the Apollo, Treadwell re-crowned the Crowns and made them the new Drifters.

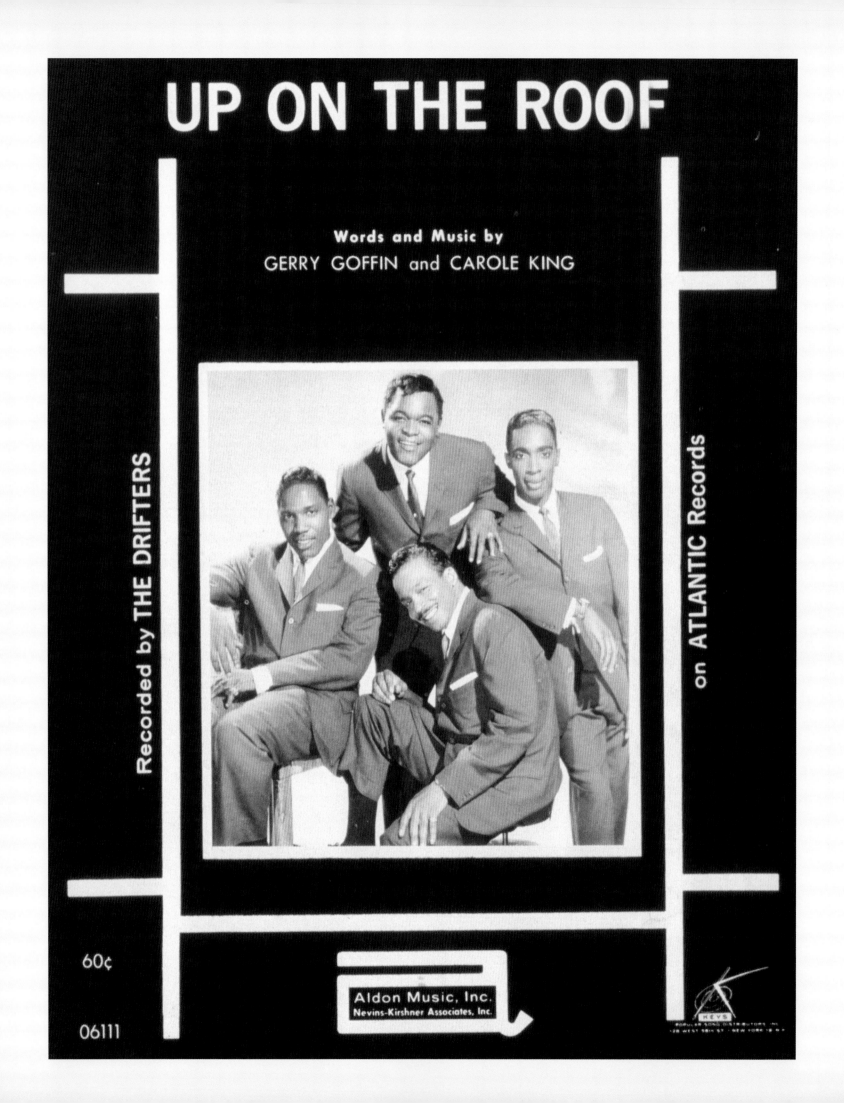

The former Crowns immediately went out on tour singing old Drifters tunes, and audiences never even realized the lineup had changed completely. Those crowds loved the lead vocalist, too, another high tenor named Bill Nelson. You know him better by the name he later chose: Ben E. King.

Ben E. King's Drifters broke new ground by incorporating strings and Latin percussion on "There Goes My Baby," which reached #2 on the R&B chart. Led by King, they went on to record a string of pearls including "This Magic Moment," "I Count the Tears," and "Save the Last Dance for Me" before King left in 1959 (even though the group was referred to as "Ben E. King's Drifters" for years). King wanted out of his relationship with Treadwell and reportedly needed to make more money than Drifters Inc. would pay him. By 1960 Treadwell had found a replacement in Rudy Lewis.

Say what you want about him, Mr. Treadwell had ears for years. With Rudy Lewis he secured another incredible run of chart-topping hits for his group. It's Lewis on those Drifters tunes we can all sing word for word: "Some Kind of Wonderful," "Up on the Roof," "Please Stay" and "On Broadway."

The last real bombshell fell on the Drifters almost exactly six years after that night at the Apollo. The group was scheduled to record a terrific new tune, which promised to be a hit, on May 21, 1964. The night before the session, Lewis was found dead in his apartment. It was never clear whether he died from a drug overdose, as the police suspected, or whether he had choked to death on an eating binge. Incredibly, the band still kept the session. Johnny Moore, who'd been singing second tenor, stepped up to the microphone that day and sang "Under the Boardwalk."

The Drifters resonated with an unprecedented fan base simply because their sound was sweet, soft and soulful. With the help of tunes penned by the famous Leiber and Stoller songwriting team, they straddled an audience that spanned gospel and pop, black and white, and from U.S. shores clear across the pond to England. They were adored and copied by Elvis Presley, Sam Cooke, Berry Gordy (of Motown Records fame) and Smokey Robinson. Heck, they even gave Dionne Warwick her start singing backup. It's that dreamy Drifters sound you want to hear whether you're up on the roof, on Broadway or on a blanket with your baby.

THE PENGUINS

Quick: sing a few lines of the 1956 single "Hey Señorita." Can't do it? Well, you're not alone. But you could probably repeat every note of its B-side, because the flip of that obscure cut is the gargantuan rock 'n' roll ballad "Earth Angel."

Dootone label owner Dootsie Williams was sure "Hey Señorita" was the A-side that would break the Penguins. When Hollywood disc jockey Dick "Huggy Boy" Hugg played both sides of the record, the phones at KGFJ radio lit up like a Christmas tree—and every call was for "Earth Angel."

For a song that arguably goes down in history as the most famous oldie of all time, "Earth Angel" had modest beginnings. For starters, no one is quite sure who wrote it—various lines have been traced back to several older songs, including Patti Page's "I Went to Your Wedding" and "Dream Girl" by Jesse Belvin and Marvin Phillips.

Enough songwriters have laid claim to the song that it has been the subject of a string of lawsuits.

When the pieces of the composition finally did fall into place, it was recorded in a Los Angeles garage on a one-track machine (reportedly at 2190 West 30th Street—good luck finding that on your map of the stars!). Legend has it that the Penguins required several takes to record the song since a neighbor's dog kept barking every time they hit the record button. It was intended to be a demo, after all, but the song exploded nationally before a more refined version ever made it to tape. One lasting bit of evidence is how abruptly the mass-produced version of the song begins. The quality of the original opening was so poor that producers lopped off the first five seconds.

of a kid who desperately wants to learn to sing bass: *Mr. Bass Man, you've got that certain somethin' / Mr. Bass Man, you set that music thumpin'*…In the song, Johnny gets a lesson from the real bass man on the recording, Ronnie Bright, who sang for the Valentines and the Cadillacs and had a delicious, low voice. Johnny never quite hits that low scat like Ronnie does, but the song is emblematic of just how cool bass singers were considered to be—"the hidden kings of rock 'n' roll," as the song goes.

Vocalists of the day all bowed respectfully to music idioms of the past, and each group had its own way of incorporating the gospel, spiritual, blues and jazz at their roots. But they also helped shape the R&B to come as they strayed from tried-and-true formulas to inject the music with truly soulful singing and fixed rhythmic patterns. At the same time, they often incorporated Tin Pan Alley song structures and driving beats (especially on uptempo numbers) that laid the groundwork for rock 'n' roll.

One distinct characteristic was that vocal groups of the early '50s typically tackled their parts with very minimal instrumental backing. Some groups, like the Larks, were accompanied by a single acoustic guitar, while others used little more than a piano or some basic percussion. Backgrounds flush with horns or orchestral accompaniment were still a few years out, not because the groups couldn't swing it artistically, but simply because there wasn't much change jingling around in their pockets. Recording budgets barely paid for studio time, so how could they afford to pay a bandstand full of union-scale musicians? Remember, it didn't cost

TV Dinners
Off with Your Aprons!

Turkey with gravy, mashed potatoes and peas. Who would have thought this simple meal, neatly packaged in aluminum trays, frozen and ready to heat, would become a kitchen phenomenon. Though frozen food was not new, when Swanson cleverly introduced its turkey combo in 1953 with the phrase "TV Dinner," a star was born. No longer slaves to the kitchen, mothers could put a hot meal on the table—or TV trays—in a fraction of the time spent creating one from scratch. Never mind that the preservatives needed would probably raise eyebrows today; TV dinners were a big hit, and paved the way for countless frozen concoctions, including desserts, added in 1960.

Marilyn Monroe

A great deal has been written and said about Marilyn Monroe, but one of the things that's easy to miss if you weren't there is that she seemed somehow fragile. Yes, she was blonde and gorgeous and Rubenesque, but her draw was her vulnerability. We had the sense that she needed to be taken care of, and that's why she played well even to our parents. While Dad's intentions might have been questionable, Mom could see something sweet and childlike in her. Everyone always thinks of Marilyn Monroe as male property, but Norma Jean needed to be mothered.

Of course, we had no idea just how fragile she really was, and how sadly in need of a real family. Years later, the veil of Hollywood would be pulled back and we'd learn how she grew up fatherless and that her mother couldn't take care of her. She was shuffled between foster care and orphanages until her first marriage at 16 years old. She really did need a mother, and the best America could offer was the warmth of the spotlight.

In 1953, a big year for Marilyn's career, she emblazoned a classic image on our culture singing "Diamonds Are a Girl's Best Friend" in *Gentlemen Prefer Blondes*, and her own dumb-blonde stereotype was burned in with *How To Marry A Millionaire*. More than half a century later, America still clings to those models of sex and beauty.

Stop a kid on the street today and he may never have heard of *Bus Stop* or Arthur Miller or the hottest 25 seconds of "Happy Birthday" ever sung, but he recognizes Monroe's image and equates it with sensuality and glamour. She has become far more than a sex symbol—Marilyn Monroe *is* beauty.

It was later that same year, 1953, that Marilyn appeared nude in the December issue of *Playboy*. Publisher Hugh Hefner had purchased and printed some racy photos taken early in her modeling career (when asked what she had on at that photo shoot, she replied, "The radio"). The pictures were considered shocking and pornographic—though today we see as much on prime time television. The famous calendar picture wasn't especially revealing, really, but for some people there was an element of disappointment in seeing her exposed. She was beautiful, of course, but now reality had taken the place of imagination. In a way, I think that was the essence of everyone's experience with her. We turned her from a person into a symbol, plastering her replica on magazine covers and movie posters and kitschy Warhol canvases. The brave new world found in Marilyn Monroe its icon of sexuality and beauty. But in reality, all we did was borrow the pretty face of a sad little girl.

The Castells

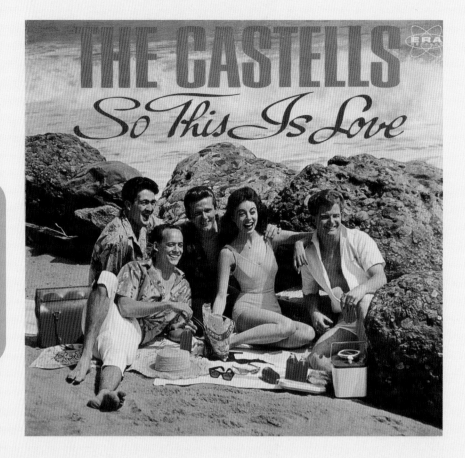

Pioneers of the early Philadelphia sound. Little more than pre-teens when they started singing on street corners, the Castells jockeyed schoolwork and studio time to produce a string of modest hits including "Marcella" and "Do You Remember."

The Cardinals

One of the best groups to come out of Baltimore, this talented quintet is remembered as a consummate blend of balladeers. Though they never achieved the stardom they deserved, their smooth and distinctive style influenced many doo wop acts who followed them.

The Harptones

New York was the breeding ground for countless doo wop stars, but sometimes the Big Apple groups—even the most talented ones—never made it to the national stage. Such was the case for the Harptones. Formed by the union of uptown and downtown singers, they were a quintessentially urban group who honed their sound in the natural reverb chamber of the Manhattan Bridge underpass.

The Harptones were led by vocalist Willie Winfield and had a secret weapon in the songwriting skills of organist Raoul J. Cita (originally of the Skylarks). Their arrangements featured five-part, jazz-inflected harmonies combined with good pop sensibility. Yet, the Harptones never had a Top 40 hit.

If the group was relegated to regional success, it was no fault of their own. Following a well-received performance at the famed Apollo Theater, the boys were invited to audition at the offices of major label MGM Records. MGM might have had the muscle to push the Harptones into the mainstream, but they never got the chance: the owners of Bruce Records, who had offices down the hall from MGM, heard the boys practicing in the hallway and signed them on the spot. But Bruce would soon fumble the ball. The Harptones gave them "A Sunday Kind of Love" during Christmas of 1953 and followed with "Memories of You" early in 1954, but the small label lacked adequate distribution. When the group signed with Old Town subsidiary Paradise Records in 1955, Cita offered up his gorgeous original "Life Is But a Dream"—but Paradise never responded with the promotion necessary to break the song outside of New York. In retrospect it seems all too appropriate that the Harptones closed out the year—and their Paradise deal—with "My Success (It All Depends on You)."

Bad business can trip up a career, but it can't stop good talent. Beautiful songs continued to flow through Cita's pen and silky tones from William's magnificent voice. Unless you had an ear pinned to New York radio—or caught one of their barnstorming performances at the Apollo—you probably missed out. Thank heaven for re-issued records.

The Clovers

It's not surprising to find, on the label of most any doo-wop hit, a writing credit that names a producer, deejay or record-industry wonk. Claiming credit for someone else's work is an unfortunate truth of the era. So it's quite a pleasant surprise to learn that industry mogul Ahmet Ertegun really did write eight of the Clovers' first nine singles, including their first number-one hits "Don't You Know I Love You" and "Fool, Fool, Fool." But don't strain your eyes looking for Ertegun's credit on the Clovers singles. Just look for the name Nugetre—that is, Ertegun spelled backwards.

Ertegun may have helped shaped the group's sound with his own compositions, but his greater gift was in nurturing their natural talent. After all, the young chief of Atlantic Records was not even a musician himself; he would record his melodies as solo vocal tracks in a Times Square recording booth, then bring the bare-bones ideas to the players. From that point it was all up to the Clovers. And boy, did they deliver.

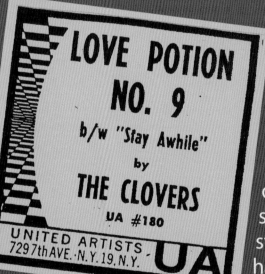

With and without the magic "Nugetre" pen at work, they ruled the early 1950s and became one of the most successful groups of the entire decade. Following "Don't You Know" and "Fool," they set up residence high on the charts. Hits to follow included "In the Middle of the Night," "One Mint Julep," "Ting-A-Ling," "Wonder Where My Baby's Gone," "Good Lovin'" and "Blue Velvet." In at least four instances, both the A- and B-sides of Clovers releases were major hits. In all, they charted twenty-one times.

Heavily influenced by the Ravens and the Ink Spots, in their heart of hearts the Clovers were an R&B group. But once they achieved huge pop success, their R&B fan base started to fall away. The group had one last gasp in 1959, when songwriters Jerry Leiber and Mike Stoller gave a Coasters-like treatment to "One Mint Julep" resulting in "Love Potion No. 9." That elixir sent them for an unprecedented run up the pop charts before they faded into doo-wop history.

The Crows

There's a story that has been passed on through generations of radio personalities. According to the legend, rock 'n' roll might not be where it is today were it not for a lovers' spat. It seems there was a deejay in California who received a copy of "Gee," a bouncin' blues tune from a little-known act called the Crows. The deejay didn't care for it and tossed the single in the trash bin, as we deejays used to do years ago with so many records (unfairly, I fully admit). The story goes that his girlfriend plucked it out of the studio's trash, played it, and fell in love with the record.

When the deejay and his girlfriend had a fight sometime later, the girlfriend stormed off and wouldn't come back. Knowing she loved "Gee," the deejay found another copy and played it over the air—repeatedly and relentlessly—until she said, "I give up! Thank you for playing my record, I'm coming back."

Thanks to the repeated airplay (which, by the way, could get a deejay fired), "Gee" started selling like wildfire. Music history was changed because in this tune were the seeds of rock 'n' roll. It was a fun song set to an uptempo beat, with a lyric pleading for a girl's attention. It had a memorable chorus, and it was easy to sing along with—it even had a guitar solo. Most important, the harmonies were tight but still had some "street" in them; in fact, the Crows were quite literally a group of street singers, having developed their sound while huddled together on a Harlem corner. To this day, a link to the street—to the everyday nitty-gritty—is the basis for credibility in rock 'n' roll music. The version of "Gee" that the Crows cut in 1953 might lack the fidelity we hear in modern recordings, but there's no mistaking the beating heart of rock 'n' roll.

anything for these groups to get started with their singing in church halls and on street corners. Every step after that was uphill.

They took chances, they improvised, they let their hearts sing. Part of the new generation's magic was that they managed to offer their music in a way that was both familiar and adventuresome.

Trade

Recording artists today wield a lot of power in the music trade. Fortified by managers, agents and lawyers, they can secure record deals that protect their rights and cover their assets. It's still true today, as it was in the early 1950s, that being signed to a record label is the Holy Grail for an aspiring performer, but back in those days most vocal groups had no one looking out for their best interests. With stars in their eyes, they routinely signed over their rights and royalties for a shot at the big time; and what they considered "big time" was rarely very big at all. Most doo wop singers would have only modest success and recognition in their own hometown, even if one single of the many they recorded hit the national charts.

Innocence was part of their charm, but naiveté would be the undoing of most doo wop groups, at least in financial terms. They were lambs on the hillside, and it was inevitable that packs of wolves would come calling. On the upside, though, even the exploitation of these young artists was evidence that there was talent and momentum on which to build a business.

The managers and start-up labels who represented the early vocal groups gave new

Naiveté would be the undoing of most doo wop groups.

THE MOONGLOWS

Shining brightly through doo wop's peak years, the Moonglows offered a warm and blended sound that made an indelible impression on rhythm & blues. During their tenure, and for decades to follow, fellow artists admired and emulated the *ooh's* and *ahh's* ("blow harmonies") that poured into every crevice of the Moonglows' refined vocal arrangements. Talent runs in the blood, they say, and the Moonglows are a credible example: Harvey Fuqua, a leader and founding member of the Moonglows, is the nephew of the Ink Spots' Charlie Fuqua. In fact, Harvey continued the family legacy of R&B greatness when he married Gwen Gordy, sister of Motown founder Berry Gordy Jr.

The Moonglows were from Cleveland, Ohio, and it was their good fortune that the city was also home to a deejay who would become one of the era's most famous personalities. As the story goes, back in 1952 the group was playing Cleveland clubs under the name the Crazy Sounds. The jazzy harmonies so impressed one club-goer that he ran to the phone, called his friend at WJW radio and held out the handset for his friend to hear. The performance transcended the low quality of the phone connection and blew away the disc jockey listening on the other end. That deejay was radio legend Alan Freed.

Freed urged the band to come down to his studio and record "I Just Can't Tell No Lie" for his own Champagne label—and then promptly launched the cut across his own airwaves. Alan "Moondog" Freed, as he was known at the time, was going to exact a fee, too, and one way was to claim writer's credit on the tune. Though his compositional contributions were few and far between, Freed attached his pen name, Al Lance, to many of the Moonglows' hits for years to come. Even after the band left his Champagne label, Freed "Lanced" many of their hits, including "Baby Please," "Whistle My Love" and "I Was Wrong" for Chicago's Chance label, and "Sincerely" for Chess. While instrumental to their success, Freed's meddling in the Moonglows' financial affairs is emblematic of how a music industry pro could exploit doo wop artists when his power went unchecked.

Depending on whom you ask, the name "Moonglows" was motivated either by a vainglorious move on Freed's part, as it echoed his Moondog nickname, or a business-savvy decision by the group to capitalize on Freed's notoriety. It was a great name either way, capturing both the softness and warmth of the group's vocals and an evening spent in the romantic light of a doo wop melody.

Diners
Chrome and Neon Palaces

KEVIN BACON, MICKEY ROURKE, DANIEL STERN AND TIMOTHY DALY IN DINER

Glittering like elongated neon jukeboxes, 1950s diners were natural teenage hang outs. We have always had an affair with jukeboxes—the chrome, lights and bubbles that emanated from every diner corner made kids feel that this was their place. Like the drive-in or the local hop, diners symbolized freedom, and breaking out of the "square" parental box.

meaning to the phrase "small-time." Though the groups may have had enormous talent, they were not going to be a big draw for the big labels—chiefly because the racial barrier had yet to be broken down. Knowing the bands wouldn't get much radio play—and therefore had limited capacity to sell records—the major labels weren't interested in the potential of black singers. But one man can make a meal of what another throws away, and home-grown record labels cropped up in the urban neighborhoods where vocal music thrived. Anyone with a connection to the musicians—a relative, a booking agent, a disc jockey—and modest resources could take a shot at running a band's career. Doo wop history is littered with tales of back-alley deals and handshake arrangements. The Del-Vikings, for instance, got their start after a talent show in Pittsburgh, Pennsylvania. The group wasn't paid a dime for their performance, but deejay Buddy Kaye was there and loved what he heard. He cornered the guys after the show and immediately brought them down to his tiny, ill-equipped basement studio, where they recorded their first singles while shoved into corners and closets.

Most of the labels were family-run businesses with limited resources, operating out of the home—call them kitchen companies, to coin a phrase. For five or ten thousand dollars, just about anyone could set up a crude version of a record label. That may not sound like much money—and it may have represented someone's life savings—but it was enough to get a group in the studio and press a few hundred records. Whoever was running the label might then ask their sister (or their mother, or their cousin) to run copies of

THE CHORDS

The Chords seemed destined for great things, yet they would all but disappear after one giant hit.

Originally calling themselves the Keynotes, the five members were well-schooled in jazz and swing, making for a more educated vocal approach than their contemporaries who drew heavily on gospel and blues. The Chords were no street-corner group, and they wanted listeners to know it. They incorporated a variety of musical styles and knew how to wrap them up in one neat pop package.

It was March of 1954 when the group went into the studio and recorded "Sh-Boom," a self-penned tune that had been originally slated as a B-side. In fact, when the Atlantic label first learned that there was heavy demand for the single, they assumed it was based on the A-side; the label had banked on the band's sophisticated read of Patti Page's "Cross Over the Bridge." Atlantic quickly changed tack, issuing "Sh-Boom" as the A-side and a new Chords track on side B.

The song rocketed up the charts. "Sh-Boom" had a sound that was very foreign at the time, but it was catchy and strong enough to draw listeners back again and again. It was novel—almost gimmicky, with the heart-beating *sh-boom* refrain and odd *ya-de-de da-de-de* repeats. Yet, in the Chords' hands, it had depth. The Crew Cuts, too, had a big hit with their cover of "Sh-Boom" that same year, and to this day a debate lingers among doo wop fans about who had the better version.

That autumn, the Chords were forced to change their name due to a legal conflict. They toiled as the Chordcats for a time before grasping at their fading fame by renaming themselves the Sh-Booms.

The Chords may not be well known, but "Sh-Boom" goes down in history with high honors. Not only was the track one of rock 'n' roll's earliest cuts, but it was the first song by a rhythm and blues group to crack the Top 10 of the pop charts.

Alan Freed Bridges the Color Barrier

Back in July of 1951, when the voice of Alan "Moondog" Freed first came over the airwaves of WJW radio in Cleveland, Ohio, there was still a huge divide between black and white music. Songs recorded by black musicians were still considered "race music." They were relegated to the race sections of music stores and saw little if any airplay on white stations. Black stations, as you might imagine, were few and far between.

Alan Freed changed all that. He knew the broadcasting bigots were wrong and refused to go along with the status quo. He did what he believed was morally and commercially right, playing rhythm & blues for an ever-growing listenership. As the audience grew, the commercials came; and with the commercials came the money. The program directors who had shunned music by black artists shrank away when Freed revealed the new truth: Not

only did audiences want to hear the music, but it was good for business.

Many listeners even thought that this pioneering champion of R&B was black himself. He was the first guy who actually sounded like the music. He had the beat in his voice, like the contagious and exciting pulse that fired up the songs he played, and audiences swarmed to him. Less than a year after he started at WJW, he hosted the "Moondog Coronation Ball" at the Cleveland Arena. To Freed's shock—and everyone else's—more than 20,000 fans, most of them black, crashed through the doors to get into the arena that night. Many consider that to be the first rock concert ever.

In 1954, when Freed made his move to radio station WINS in New York, he had to drop his nickname. The story behind that is quintessential New York City, too: There was a blind street musician in Manhattan whose real name was Louis Hardin, but he went by the name Moondog. Hardin was a fixture on Sixth Avenue, and he'd hand out songs and poetry for money. He was quite a sight, too: He had a long beard and mustache, wore a cape and sandals, always wore a Viking helmet and carried a big spear. People thought Hardin was probably homeless, but every now and then I used to see a car pick him up at the end of his day! He must have had some significant resources since he was able to prevent Freed from using the nickname Moondog on the air. Years later, New Yorkers learned that Hardin was actually an accomplished composer who conducted in Europe and recorded for several major labels. It's a testament to Freed's good heart that he even played some of Hardin's work on his own show.

ALAN FREED

"ROCK N ROLL"

SECOND ANNIVERSARY

Credit for coining the phrase "rock 'n' roll" often goes to Freed, but he didn't invent it so much as adopt it. "Rock and roll" was a black slang term from back in the 1920s, a euphemism for sex. Then it took on broader connotations based on how gospel music would literally make people move—they'd be rockin' and rollin'. Freed rediscovered the slang and used it to describe the new music.

Freed's name became synonymous with rock 'n' roll, and he was the first major personality to be identified with the music through radio, television and movies. He started his own record labels, signed artists and promoted concerts. But as the rock 'n' roll machine grew bigger and bigger, Freed got caught up in its cogs. There were some negative influences in the growing music industry, and I believe Freed took bad advice from some of the people around him. He paid a heavy price both professionally and personally. By 1960, most stations wouldn't touch him. It was a sad ending to a great career, and in 1965 he passed away from kidney failure and liver cirrhosis.

Alan Freed's career did not end as nobly as it began, but he bridged a gap that changed pop music forever. Without him, doo wop may never have crossed over and reached the masses. Alan Freed gets the gold medal for that one.

The Charms

It seems strange now, but for years it was common for more than one group to be on the charts with the same song. When it came to slugging it out over cover songs, the Charms proved themselves to be quite a scrappy little gang. Unfortunately, there was also contention within the group itself.

Hailing from Cincinnati, the Charms were originally a sextet led by vocalist Otis Williams (not the same Otis Williams of the Temptations, by the way), and beginning in 1953 they were off to a strong start with a run of original songs. In September of 1954 they took a shot at "Hearts of Stone," releasing their cover just one week after the Jewels released the original. The Charms won out, besting the Jewels' chart position—but were themselves trumped by yet another version, recorded by the Fontanes.

Cover competition became part and parcel of the Charms' career, including "Ling, Ting, Tong" (with which the Five Keys had a bigger hit); "Ko Ko Mo," which was released in 1955 by no less than five groups; and "Two Hearts," which launched a seemingly endless string of hits—not for the Charms, unfortunately, but for Pat Boone.

Deluxe, the group's record label, saw Otis as the big draw. In fact, when the rest of the Charms asked for a raise in wages, Deluxe summarily fired them all except Otis. In the years that followed, multiple claims to the Charms name made it tricky to figure out just who, exactly, fans were listening to. However, the group known as Otis Williams and His Charms received the lion's share of attention, and they are remembered for being on the bill with a few other artists in the first-ever R&B show at Carnegie Hall in 1955.

the record up to the local radio station and beg for a little airplay. They might pull a favor at the local music store and ask a friend to put the record on their shelf. The kitchen companies and the bands themselves didn't bank on much more than regional success; for many it was enough of a thrill to be heard on local radio and get a slap on the back walking through the neighborhood. With a bit of airplay, though, groups could also get booked at clubs and theaters, where they stood to make a few dollars performing.

And every now and then, they hit it right. Sometimes it took little more than a supportive deejay or a great gig for the spark to catch, and before anyone knew it the whole town would be singing along. That's what happened when fortune shone on the Moonglows. Playing a free gig at the Centerfield Lounge in Cleveland, one fan was so excited he called the local deejay and held out the phone as the group sang onstage. Those beautiful harmonies blew right through the telephone line, and the disc jockey wanted the group to come to his studio after their show. He was quick to capture the band on tape and release their first single, "I Just Can't Tell No Lie." That deejay was Alan Freed, and he launched a long, successful career for the Moonglows.

If a group could create just enough fuss with a solid tune, they would fill theater seats and expand their reach on radio. Right about then, a major label would start to sniff a little green in the air. That's when the major would swoop in and offer to buy the master recording from the kitchen company. The music rights would be

The Medallions

A New Hit! "EDNA"

A foursome from Los Angeles, they scored with "The Letter" and a quirky number called "Buick '59." According to doo wop mythology, "Buick '59," released in 1954, was designed with double-duty potential: it could be re-issued in 1959!

DOOTONE
RECORDS 9512 So. Central Ave Los Angeles 2, Calif.

GIRL:
HEY JOHNNY,
WHAT ARE YOU
REBELLING AGAINST?
JOHNNY:
WHATTYA GOT?

COLUMBIA PICTURES
Presents
A STANLEY KRAMER
PRODUCTION

MARLON BRANDO as

THE WILD ONE

X

with MARY MURPHY · ROBERT KEITH
and LEE MARVIN
Screenplay by JOHN PAXTON
Directed by LASLO BENEDEK

Our nation's youth were still pretty squeaky clean in 1953. In America's breadbasket, it was all milk and apple pie. At the top of the charts was Dean Martin with "That's Amore," followed by Tony Bennett and Les Paul & Mary Ford. But just down the road you could hear the sound of engines revving.

Then, in rides Marlon Brando. As gang leader Johnny Malone in *The Wild One*, he and the Black Rebels Motorcycle Club roar into small-town America to do some wrong in Wrightsville. He's wearing a leather jacket, jeans and sunglasses—an "outlaw outfit," as they say in the film. *The Wild One* might not have been Brando's crowning achievement (*Streetcar Named Desire* came two years before, and *On The Waterfront* one year later), but it was a rock 'n' roll milestone. In his suave character, eyes half shut from boredom with the status quo, Brando created the icon of the American rebel. It was his blueprint that Elvis and James Dean would follow in the coming years.

Looking back on it now, 1953's version of "wild" seems pretty mild. The biker hat he wore looks kind of silly, and the gang's idea of being tough was to drink a bottle of beer without using a glass (gasp!). In truth, Hollywood wasn't really in the business of shocking anybody. Brando was no street urchin—he was Hollywood's idea of a rough-and-ready type. They wanted someone right in the middle, someone who would appeal to young people but not frighten Mom and Dad too much.

Still, *The Wild One* really embodied the rock 'n' roll spirit to come. It was about doing what you wanted and going wherever the wind blew you. "Staying in one place, that's cornball stuff," says Johnny. "You've got to go." More than anyone had before, Brando embodied a new attitude and the look to go with it. He let everyone know he was going to live his life exactly as he wanted. That's what this movie was all about: Freedom.

The Diablos

On a first listen to the Diablos, R&B fans can be forgiven for mistaking vocalist Nolan Strong for a young Smokey Robinson. Both have gentle, airy voices that effortlessly skip through the upper range of high tenor, and both are achingly romantic. Smokey was just a teen, in fact, when he first heard Nolan, and at fourteen years old formed a pick-up vocal group to imitate the leads he heard on the Diablos' first single, "Adios, My Desert Love."

The Strong/Robinson connection was part of a great vocal legacy, as Nolan had been inspired by the last great tenor before himself, Clyde McPhatter.

The Diablos were just about to record their first demos in a Detroit studio when its owners, Devora and Jack Brown, signed them to their own Fortune label. Following "Adios," the group was swept away with the success of "The Wind" late in 1954. Such a hit was the airy track (later covered by the Jesters) that the fledgling Fortune could barely handle national-scale demands. Fronted by Strong's unique and mesmerizing stylings, the Diablos enjoyed a brief two years of praise by fans and critics before Strong joined the army at the end of 1956. The group resumed in 1959 and stuck with Fortune their whole career, but all memories of them are carried on "The Wind."

bought out by the bigger label for bigger bucks; the kitchen company would recoup whatever money had been laid out; and the vocal group—remember the vocal group?—just might have a shot at the national spotlight.

Technology

Much of the nuance and beauty in vocal music would have gone right by our ears were it not for advances in audio technology. In fact, if the recording and playback equipment hadn't been in place to recreate this music with the clarity it deserved, doo wop might never have been noticed at all.

The march of progress had for a long time been slowed by the march of war. During the years we were fighting World War II, America poured all its resources into the military, and technology that catered to civilian luxuries just had to wait. FM radio, for example, was developed in the '40s but it was well over a decade before music lovers were enjoying FM music broadcasts. On the other hand, the war helped introduce new ideas such as recording music magnetically on tape, a technique we "borrowed" when the U.S. Army raided a German radio station.

By the time vocal groups began descending on local studios, recording gear had stepped up a few notches. The microphones in use at the time were of very high quality, with great range and frequency response (in fact, the tube electronics and precision craftsmanship of those microphones make them worth thousands of dollars to today's record producers). Studios made the most of those

Music was the prize; technology was the box it came in.

The Flamingos

Elegance and sophistication are the words that come to mind in describing the Flamingos. There was a precision and perfection to their harmonies that no other doo wop group rivaled. But we all know that quality doesn't always equate with popularity. As beautiful and refined as the Flamingos' sound was, it didn't appeal to everybody, and their talent was never rewarded with the commercial success they deserved.

"I Only Have Eyes for You," released in the summer of 1959, was the Flamingos' big hit. With its love-drunk lead and *shoo-bop shoo-bop* vocal catch, the song is a good representation of their sound: skilled, orchestrated and dreamily romantic. Nobody played "make out" music better than this group, and their catalog is full of slow, tender songs. The Flamingos are like a musical aphrodisiac. To some people's ears, though, Flamingos love songs are almost too rich and sweet. Like a box of chocolates, you love 'em but you can't take too much all at once.

Oldies stations may play "I Only Have Eyes" till the end of time, but "Golden Teardrops" was truly the Flamingos' landmark cut. Released about six years prior, in the fall of 1953, this track is known to

aficionados of vocal harmony as the most perfect-sounding single of all time. The performance on it is nothing short of masterful.

Motown and other R&B groups who followed in the '60s have credited the Flamingos as a major influence. They were among very few doo wop groups who came on the scene with a cappella vocal training and then went on to play instruments—arguably making them the first R&B vocal unit equipped to accompany itself. Yet another layer of the Flamingos' talent came in the form of choreography. It may seem counter-intuitive that a group with unparalleled vocal skill would put much energy into a stage act, but maybe they incorporated dancing to offset their talent. Maybe they were too good, and had to bring a little bit of circus into their act to broaden their appeal.

Record collectors and music critics hold the Flamingos up as being the best of the best. But what makes a group "the best"? A sound that becomes a huge hit with the masses, or top-shelf talent that appeals to a small audience of connoisseurs? That was the problem with the Flamingos. Their enormous talent was both a blessing and a burden. One has to admit, though—it's a nice problem to have.

The FLAMINGOS

`Golden Teardrops' was considered a perfect vocal recording if ever there was one.

mics, too. Rather than gathering the whole group around one microphone, engineers started setting up baffles in the studio and having each singer record his part discretely. The final recordings featured clean separation between the lead singer, the midrange voices, and the bass. With well-separated vocal tracks, pristine performances like the Flamingos' "Golden Teardrops"—considered a perfect vocal recording if ever there was one—could be appreciated in all their glory.

All that great gear would mean nothing going into a recording if we had no way to hear it playing back out. By halfway through the last century, audio electronics had come a long way from the original Gramophones, and it was common to find a big ol' phonograph console in the family living room playing back the heavy hunks of black shellac we called records—78-rpm records, to be specific. But what really made a difference to the history of popular music was not how records and turntables recreated the subtleties of the human voice. The change came with affordability and portability.

Miniaturization is very popular today. It's evident in everything from microcomputers and nano technology, to our cars to our credit cards. When we can carry more of our stuff around with us, we feel free and untied to any one place. Record players had been fixtures in the home. It was Mom and Dad's player, and if you were lucky they spun a few records you liked. When manufacturers like Decca made players that could be unplugged, packed up, and brought to a friend's house, it was a crucial step in untethering teenagers from their parents' world. And when portable players for the smaller, 45-rpm

The Five Keys

The Five Keys had just one big hit in "Glory of Love," which had been a #1 song for Benny Goodman back in 1936. Yet for some reason they captured our imaginations. We appreciate them more today and in retrospect can also appreciate how influential they were upon their peers.

For fans who do know the group, "Glory," "Ling, Ting, Tong" and "Close Your Eyes" are the singles that leap to mind. In any sampling of Five Keys music, their singular talent is evident. They poured everything into their music—gospel, R&B, jazz, pop—and mixed it all up beautifully.

"Ling, Ting, Tong" was covered a number of times, notably by Bill Haley and by Otis Williams and the Charms. The song is sort of a red herring for the Five Keys. Here you have an immensely talented group with three of the finest lead singers in doo wop—Maryland Pierce, Dickie Smith and Rudy West—knocking out a silly song with a chorus that imitates Asian talking. But even in this novelty throwaway it's clear that the Five Keys could bring the sheen of perfection and professionalism to any musical undertaking.

2 Great Capitol Records Releases.
Published by
KAHL MUSIC, INC.
1619 Broadway,
New York 19, New York

THE FIVE KEYS singing "THE VERDICT"
Capitol-3127
b/w "WE MAKE-UM POW POW"

THE CASH BOX
AWARD O' THE WEEK
The Billboard • This Week's Best
VARIETY • Best Bets

DAKOTA STATON singing "DON'T LEAVE ME NOW"
Capitol-3128
b/w "A LITTLE YOU"

Edward R. Murrow Brings the News Home

Widely credited with inventing broadcast television news, Edward R. Murrow was a seminal figure in American journalism. In a career that spanned twenty-five years, Murrow's distinctive voice was first heard on the radio, particularly his frontline reporting from the Battle of Britain. By 1951 he was quick to seize the potential power of television, and began hosting *See It Now*, a news show that set the mold for countless documentary-style programs to follow. With his ever-present cigarette, Murrow was welcomed into living rooms as a trusted commentator on critical issues, and paved the way for the broadcast heavyweights to come.

singles became affordable, it was much more than a fad—it was the beginning of an unstoppable youth movement.

The 45-rpm record represented independence day for young people. Talk about revolutions per minute—it was like every new single changed a teenager's life. Freedom! Now all the music that resonated so strongly, the songs that made them laugh and cry and dance and scream, was part of a moveable feast. Jukeboxes were loaded with "45's," too, and the singles that blared from jukes in soda shops, watering holes and restaurants could be shared by teenyboppers as they listened on their bedroom floors. Portable radios, now small and light enough to tote around the parking lots and roller rinks, were also little magic music makers. Of course, technology was just part of the formula. Music was the prize; technology was the box it came in.

Here at the crossroads of "the three T's," things were changing. Society's eye was shifting its glance towards youth. No one realized it at the time, but the doo wop groups were about to hit their creative peak just as the power balance was shifting to their young audience. How could they miss?

Like most of the world's young people, America's youth were gathering strength as if someone had planned a peaceful *coup d'état* of pop culture. The takeover wouldn't be complete for years to come, but the year 1954 marked a turning point from which American culture has never looked back. From the kids' perspective, it looked like liberation. From their parents' perspective, it looked like a generation gone mad. And from the perspective of big business, it looked like opportunity.

THE PLATTERS

CHAPTER 4
1955-1956

Big Business Takes Over

For the first time in history, youth was poised to dominate the lifestyle of the masses. Beginning in the mid 1950s, and continuing to this day, the passions and interests of the young would steer popular culture. The torch wasn't passed to them—it was pried from the hands of moms and dads, a generation that was losing its grip in more ways than one. An enormous reserve of musical talent was building, a fresh new 25-and-under market was waiting with open arms, and record companies were beginning to tap its enormously expanded potential. Rock 'n' roll had appeared on the horizon, and it was galloping fast toward Everytown, USA. That's when big business rolled up its sleeves and started punching calculators.

Cultural sea changes don't happen overnight; even the most dramatic shifts have an evolutionary history. In music, the older generation had already cocked its ear in curiosity—or in disgust—when vocalist Johnnie Ray was heard among the milquetoast pop singers of the early '50s. Ray nearly caused a revolution all on his own. Here was a guy singing otherwise palatable songs like "Cry" and "Walkin' My Baby Back Home," but delivering them in an eerie, otherworldly voice. Ray was nearly deaf and seldom held a note for long; rather, he would clip a melody note short after a rapid rise and fall. He was just as famous for his strange vocal approach as for writhing on the stage floor and breaking down in tears. Doris Day must have passed out cold.

Rock 'n' roll had appeared on the horizon, and it was galloping fast toward Everytown, USA.

performers like Frankie Laine ("That Lucky Old Sun"), Eileen Barton ("If I Knew You Were Comin' I'd've Baked a Cake") and LaVern Baker ("Jim Dandy")—infused their music with a newness and, even more importantly, a pulse that got young hearts beating fast. Teenagers had yearned for something all their own, and the beat resonated inside them from head to toe. Portable radios and phonographs had given them mobility; now, the music inspired movement within their own bodies.

To borrow Newton's famous law, a body in motion tends to stay in motion.

Popular music was being charged by a jolt of rhythmic energy, and the growing herd of vocal groups was electrified. The often placid and plaintive sounds that defined early doo wop became infused with an infectious beat. One great example of a group managing the transition from old-school to new-school doo wop is the Clovers. The quintet had scored a number of bluesy hits since 1950 and shown a penchant for rocking beats as early as 1952 with "In the Middle of the Night." Four years later, their landmark 1956 hit, "Devil or Angel," was driven by a swaying beat—and that's in a ballad. The Clovers blurred the line between vocal harmony and rock 'n' roll, and it was fundamental to their success.

In 1955 and 1956, rockin' rhythms propelled the best doo wop. The Del-Vikings hit with "Come Go with Me," the Cleftones had "Little Girl of Mine" and "Can't We Be Sweethearts," and the El Dorados thumped away on "At My Front Door" and its sequel, "Bim Bam Boom."

The Drifters proved themselves to be masters at navigating every style in every decade of their career. In January of 1955 they were headlining Alan

FRANKIE LYMON AND THE TEENAGERS

James Dean

James Dean has become such an icon that his image keeps drifting further and further from who he really was. Not that any of us could have known him very well:; he died at age twenty-four, and his legend is built around the roles he played in a mere three films. Dean lives on in our minds as the prototypical rebel, in jeans and a white tee shirt with cigarettes rolled into the sleeve. But that tough-guy image isn't really consistent with Dean or even with the characters he played.

His rebellion always seemed very hard won. Unlike an invulnerable bad boy such as Marlon Brando, Dean's rebellion seemed to tear him apart from the inside out. One reason women fell head over heels for him, after all, was that he portrayed such sensitivity. Reportedly, Dean brought a lot of his own Indiana upbringing to the screen in 1955's *East of Eden*, the film adaptation of John Steinbeck's novel; the strained father-son relationship on screen may have mirrored his own. Dean's character, Cal, was angry and untamed in the film, but what teenagers related to was his reaction to a wildly dysfunctional family.

The trailer for *Eden* called it "the frankest motion picture ever made," and in it Dean gave meaning to the phrase "painfully honest." Likewise, in *Rebel Without A Cause*, Dean manifests teenage pain and struggle like no one had before (though Dean himself was twenty-four by the time *Rebel* was released). Gazing up at the big screen, teenagers could watch some representation of their own battles with parents ("You're tearing me apart!") and love unfold in living color. By Dean's side were other characters for audiences to relate to. The girls wanted to stare into Jimmy's baby blues and take care of him like Natalie Wood did, as Judy. Sal Mineo, as the admiring Plato, represented the desire for camaraderie and loyalty among teenage boys—including homoerotic undertones which the studio was very careful to downplay in 1955.

Giant, Dean's final film, found him playing a more mature character: Jett Rink is still a rebel of sorts but he never learns the mistakes of his ways. Sadly, Dean died before the film was released in 1956. For many people, James Dean embodies the expression "Live fast, die young"—a notion that can sound romantic, especially in the dramatic setting of a teenager's life. But Dean shouldn't be reduced to a motto or to an icon of rebellion. He was a talented actor who gave voice to a generation, and we would have loved to hear that voice for at least a few more years.

JAMES DEAN

The Drive-In

What a thrill, what a simple pleasure it was to go to a drive-in movie! The experience brought together so many rare and cherished opportunities: to be in the car, to be entertained, to have a private place.

We can all remember the genuine excitement as the car rolled into a good spot, with the gravel crunching under the tires. With a few hours of freedom stretching out before us, the driver reached out his window, pulled the clunky metal speaker off the pole and hung it on his window. A cartoon soda cup and ice-cream sandwich would do a little dance as the flick started, urging one last trip to the refreshment center before the movie stars came alive on a thirty-foot-high screen.

The first drive-in opened way back in 1933, in Camden, New Jersey, and they began appearing all over the country in the 1940s. But the mid-1950s were their heyday. In 1956 you could roll up to see *Elvis in Love Me Tender*, James Dean in *Giant*, and Marilyn in *Bus Stop*. Drive-in buffs say the peak of operation was in 1958, when nearly five thousand drive-in theaters were playing movies all across the U.S.

One of the great things about a drive-in was that you could watch a movie and still have privacy in the comfort of your own car, like it was a living room on wheels. That made drive-ins fun for everybody. They were great for families, since the kids could watch or fall asleep in the back. Packs of friends would go in a train of cars, usually with a spare pal or two in the trunk to save on admission. And of course, there were few better places for two young lovers to go on a date. Whether it took half the movie to hold hands, or if the windows were fogged up before the second scene, there was a very special kind of romance at the drive-in. Funny how their popularity coincided with the Baby Boom, huh?

Freed's *Rock 'n' Roll Ball*, and shot up the charts with "Whatcha Gonna Do."

Excluding a handful of stars, the groups who didn't evolve fell away from the charts (a notable exception being the Five Satins, who released "Wonderful Girl" and the unparalleled "In the Still of the Night" in 1956). It was possible for a vocal group to still have a career below Billboard's radar, but the era defined by the lush and languid sound of the Flamingos, the Five Keys and the Orioles was over.

By 1955, the whole equation of vocal music had changed. The previous generation of pop audiences listened to lyrics and a melody; the new generation wanted to feel a beat. Long and wandering melodies were supplanted by short verses and choruses laden with catchy hooks. The balance of vocals and instrumentation was nearly reversed as it became routine for groups to enter the studio with a four-piece outfit of rock 'n' roll sidemen. Though doo wop singing had been based on the imitation of instruments, groups were also accompanied by string sections and horn players.

Vocal music crossed paths with rock 'n' roll rhythm and fell in love. Pressed to identify doo wop as some sort of musical offspring, you could say it was born from the marriage of these two styles: vocal harmony + rock 'n' roll = doo wop.

Radio Rolls with the Record Biz

The mid-fifties doo wop boom was due to the burgeoning relationship of radio and the record industry. Symbiosis between the two was yielding unprecedented success for both. Rock 'n' roll stars

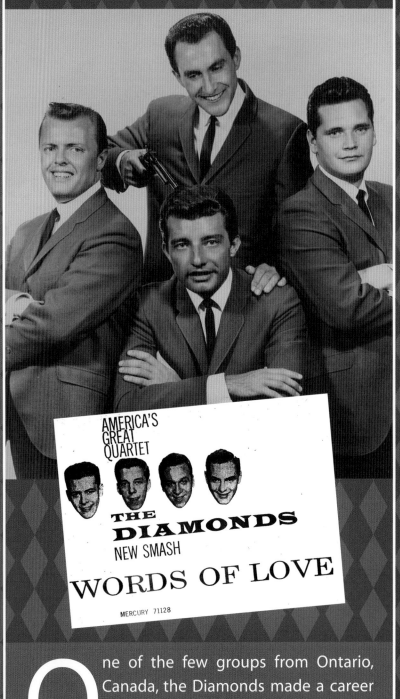

The Diamonds

AMERICA'S GREAT QUARTET

THE DIAMONDS NEW SMASH

WORDS OF LOVE

MERCURY 71128

One of the few groups from Ontario, Canada, the Diamonds made a career covering songs already released like "Why Do Fools Fall in Love," "Church Bells May Ring" and "Silhouettes." However, unlike most cover groups of the era, they knew their stuff and turned the Gladiolas' little known "Little Darlin'" into a major hit on both the pop and R&B charts. They did have one original hit, "The Stroll," in 1958.

The Robins

Navigating the road to success was a challenge for every group, and the ones who "made it" often had to weave through the obstacles of shifting personnel, short-term label deals and stiff competition. Others, like the Robins, gradually broke down along that road.

Originally a West Coast trio based in San Francisco, the Robins had been heavily influenced by bigger birds before them, namely the Ravens. They recorded for no fewer than ten labels in as many years and added three new members to their ranks before making their biggest marks in 1954 and 1955 with the Spark singles "Riot in Cell Block #9" and "Smokey Joe's Café," respectively.

Both the fate and the fortune of the group's members were tied to their relationship with songwriters Jerry Leiber and Mike Stoller. Spark was owned by the dynamic duo, and though they saw potential in the Robins, they knew the singers could really spread their wings in a different setting. Eventually, Lieber and Stoller gutted the band, shifting members Carl Gardner and Bobby Nunn to another of their interests. A worthy sacrifice? You be the judge: Gardner and Nunn were the cornerstones of the Coasters.

like Bill Haley and a hip-swinging Memphis boy named Elvis Presley were selling records faster than flapjacks, and the young doo woppers who infused their music with romping beats were welcome at the party.

The record industry had long understood, even before the Ames Brothers or Frank Sinatra, that radio play equated record sales. Naturally, the more "needle drops" a song received at radio, the more familiar it became to listeners' ears: familiarity breeds content, you might say. That philosophy had paid off for the music industry ever since the days when a store selling sheet music would hire a pianist to play on its show floor for ten hours a day.

Step one for the industry was to deluge radio programmers with new releases, so stations regularly received all the new "product" rolling off record label presses. These were the early days of record promotion, wherein label representatives would do whatever they could to implore broadcasters to spin their songs on the air. All the airplay in the world would mean nothing, though, unless listeners could go out and purchase the records at their local music shops. Ensuring there would always be supply to meet consumer demand, record distribution reached extraordinary levels of saturation. The labels stuffed store shelves with their product. The cycle of sales was self-perpetuating, too: Radio stations would call the stores to learn what their top sellers were; those charts dictated radio playlists; and then the top-selling songs would go into heavy rotation on radio, nearly guaranteeing that more

Freed's *Rock 'n' Roll Ball*, and shot up the charts with "Whatcha Gonna Do."

Excluding a handful of stars, the groups who didn't evolve fell away from the charts (a notable exception being the Five Satins, who released "Wonderful Girl" and the unparalleled "In the Still of the Night" in 1956). It was possible for a vocal group to still have a career below Billboard's radar, but the era defined by the lush and languid sound of the Flamingos, the Five Keys and the Orioles was over.

By 1955, the whole equation of vocal music had changed. The previous generation of pop audiences listened to lyrics and a melody; the new generation wanted to feel a beat. Long and wandering melodies were supplanted by short verses and choruses laden with catchy hooks. The balance of vocals and instrumentation was nearly reversed as it became routine for groups to enter the studio with a four-piece outfit of rock 'n' roll sidemen. Though doo wop singing had been based on the imitation of instruments, groups were also accompanied by string sections and horn players.

Vocal music crossed paths with rock 'n' roll rhythm and fell in love. Pressed to identify doo wop as some sort of musical offspring, you could say it was born from the marriage of these two styles: vocal harmony + rock 'n' roll = doo wop.

Radio Rolls with the Record Biz

The mid-fifties doo wop boom was due to the burgeoning relationship of radio and the record industry. Symbiosis between the two was yielding unprecedented success for both. Rock 'n' roll stars

The D

AMERICA'S GREAT QUARTET

THE DIA
NEW SMASH

WORDS

MERCURY 71128

One of the Canada, th covering "Why Do Bells May Ring" and " most cover groups of and turned the Gladio into a major hit on b They did have one ori

BIG

The Robins

Navigating the road to success was a challenge for every group, and the ones who "made it" often had to weave through the obstacles of shifting personnel, short-term label deals and stiff competition. Others, like the Robins, gradually broke down along that road.

Originally a West Coast trio based in San Francisco, the Robins had been heavily influenced by bigger birds before them, namely the Ravens. They recorded for no fewer than ten labels in as many years and added three new members to their ranks before making their biggest marks in 1954 and 1955 with the Spark singles "Riot in Cell Block #9" and "Smokey Joe's Café," respectively.

Both the fate and the fortune of the group's members were tied to their relationship with songwriters Jerry Leiber and Mike Stoller. Spark was owned by the dynamic duo, and though they saw potential in the Robins, they knew the singers could really spread their wings in a different setting. Eventually, Lieber and Stoller gutted the band, shifting members Carl Gardner and Bobby Nunn to another of their interests. A worthy sacrifice? You be the judge: Gardner and Nunn were the cornerstones of the Coasters.

like Bill Haley and a hip-sw[...] named Elvis Presley were [...] than flapjacks, and the you[...] infused their music with [...] welcome at the party.

The record industry had l[...] before the Ames Brothers [...] radio play equated record[...] more "needle drops" a song[...] more familiar it became[...] familiarity breeds content[...] philosophy had paid off f[...] ever since the days when [...] music would hire a pianist t[...] for ten hours a day.

Step one for the industry [...] programmers with new [...] regularly received all the ne[...] record label presses. These [...] record promotion, wherein[...] would do whatever the [...] broadcasters to spin their s[...] airplay in the world would n[...] unless listeners could go [...] records at their local music[...] would always be supply[...] demand, record di[...] extraordinary levels of s[...] stuffed store shelves with t[...] of sales was self-perpetuati[...] would call the stores to lear[...] were; those charts dictate[...] then the top-selling songs[...] rotation on radio, nearly g[...]

The Dells' sound is smooth and easygoing, but it's the result of a remarkable amount of work and dedication. Having started as the El-Rays outside of Chicago in 1952, they were dealt early defeats that would have spelled the end of any lesser group. Their first singles went nowhere. No one, including the Dells themselves, would have guessed they were on the front end of a career that would last half a century.

It was 1956 when "Oh What a Nite" came out on Vee-Jay Records, destined for a run to the Top 5 of the R&B charts. As the story goes, the guys were sinking some baskets outside the local schoolyard, fretting over their career, when friends came up to them all excited. "Hey, we just heard your song on the radio," they told the dumbstruck Dells. "You have a big hit!"

The Dells didn't see much more chart action in the following few years, though they released good material and took their act on the road. It would have been par for the doo wop course if the Dells had been a one-hit wonder. Most doo wop groups had peaked by 1960, but the Dells were just beginning their ascent. That year marked the departure of lead Johnny "Junior" Funches, who was replaced with Johnny Carter from the Flamingos. Incredibly, that was their last personnel change for forty years. It was also the year they began opening and singing backup for jazz legend Dinah Washington. The Dells honed their skills to sing jazz harmonies behind Washington, developing a warm and refined sound that appealed to critics and fans alike.

Resuming their own recording career, the Dells charted in 1965 with "Stay in My Corner"—nine years after "Oh What a Nite," they finally returned to the Top 30. The key to the Dells' return, though, was not cashing in on the so-called "oldies" nostalgia. Rather, the group had the talent and foresight to reinvent themselves in R&B's brave new world. After backing up Ray Charles in 1966, their career hit its pace late in the decade, and they held their own among the Supremes, Otis Redding, Sly and the Family Stone, and the Temptations. In 1969, while love children grooved to Jimi Hendrix and the Beatles' Abbey Road, the Dells hit the Top 10 with a remake of "Oh What a Nite."

The Dells just never ran out of steam. Their soothing, soulful sound earned them a dedicated fan base that sent a few singles bubbling up the charts (notably, 1973's million-selling "Give Your Baby a Standing Ovation") as they continued releasing records and selling concert seats. While most of their contemporaries were leaning back in their rocking chairs, the Dells were recording new music and getting inducted into the Rock and Roll Hall of Fame. Remaining a tightly knit unit while flowing loosely with the times proved to be a winning formula for the Dells.

The Dells

The Five Satins

L
ike so many doo wop groups, the Five Satins are known for just one song. But oh what a song it is. Few would argue that "In the Still of the Night" is the preeminent doo wop composition, if not the finest three minutes and four seconds ever recorded in fifty years of pop music.

First released in 1956, the song's romantic sway and melancholy delivery is undeniable on first listen. It was written by the group's Fred Parris when he was just nineteen years old. As Parris told the Smithsonian years later, he penned the song late one night, when the army had him stationed in Philadelphia. "It was a cold, black night, and the stars were twinkling. The setting was very apropos for my feelings and emotions." Underneath the dark sky, Parris was remembering a sweet, warm night the previous May that he had spent with a girl named Marla back near his home in New Haven, Connecticut.

Just as the song is about Parris' own treasured memory, it seems to evoke an incredibly strong feeling of reflection and nostalgia in everyone who hears it. When I was at WCBS in New York, listeners voted "In the Still of the Night" as their favorite song for twelve years straight—and that was twenty years after it was first released! To this day, "In the Still of the Night" remains a model of doo wop perfection—and a trip straight down the middle of Memory Lane.

The Nutmegs

Some groups are named after birds, some after cars, some even after animals. But why name a group after a spice? That's easy: This group is from Connecticut, the Nutmeg State! Connecticut may not exactly be remembered as the home of doo wop, but the Nutmegs weren't alone. Their fair city of New Haven was also home to the Scarlets, the Chestnuts and the Five Satins.

doo wop is famous for its cavalcade of one-hit wonders, but the Nutmegs were in fact a two-hit wonder. "Story Untold" and "Ship of Love" were first released in March and August of 1955, respectively. Though additional hits eluded the group, they were able to stay in the game by re-releasing both songs several times. A second chapter in Nutmegs history began in 1963, when they found themselves at the forefront of an unlikely a cappella craze that lasted for about three years.

A cappella (literally, "as in the chapel," meaning vocal music with no instrumental accompaniment) was a small movement but attracted a loyal audience. The brief phase was all the more unlikely since it happened at a time when rock 'n' roll music was becoming increasingly bombastic. There amidst all the "noise" were the Nutmegs with no drums, bass or rock 'n' roll swagger—just a chorus of their angelic vocals.

listeners would head to the stores with their wallets wide open. It was a nepotistic and sometimes dirty business.

Industry coffers were brimming with cash from record receipts, but little of the overflow ever made it downstream to the artists. Even in the earlier days of kitchen companies, the groups had stars in their eyes and were rarely counseled wisely by managers or agents. They were kids, after all; they were in the business for the thrill of performing, for seeing the world from a tour-bus window, and to be adored by throngs of screaming girls. Major labels would be the last to look out for the artists' best interests.

In fact, even in their heyday most doo wop groups were considered small potatoes by major labels like Capitol, MGM and RCA. The record companies would work hard to sustain the careers of idols like Eddie Fisher, Joe Stafford or the Four Aces, and got behind rock 'n' roll acts only after Elvis shook their world in 1956. But because a doo wop group was only as valuable as its last chart-topper, the majors weren't inclined to nurture their careers with marketing campaigns, publicity, movie spots or long-term contracts. On nationwide and international scales, most were destined to be faceless one-hit wonders. This goes a long way toward explaining why there are nearly as many doo wop artists as there are doo wop hits.

Still, doo wop had grown too successful to be managed by a guy stuffing cash into the kitchen cookie jar. Having been a grassroots movement since the beginning, vocal groups always sold reliably in regional markets. A cadre of independent labels took the doo wop groups under their wing

The Channels

"The Closer You Are" was just a blip on the national radar back in 1956, but the Channels were better known on the East Coast. New York born and bred, the quintet got their start like so many of their local contemporaries did: on Amateur Night at the Apollo Theater in Harlem. That famous stage provided the launch pad for umpteen doo wop groups, and while some soared over the country, others hovered over smaller regions. The Channels' ambitious five-part harmonies may have been enough to win over audiences on a broader scale, but they never had the chance to find out.

Everybody PICKS It #1 For

The Channels
"THE GLEAM I
YOUR EYES"
c/w
"STARS IN THE SKY"
Whirlin Disc #102

America's Fastest Growing R&B Label

WHIRLIN DISC

315 W. 47 St., N. Y.
(PL 7-8140)

Detroit Goes Rock 'n' Roll

Cars equal freedom. Even today, any teenager lucky enough to snag Dad's wheels for a few hours can glimpse the timeless appeal that romanticized the fabulous autos of the doo wop era. They embody our love of exploration, a chance to go where we want at our will and whim. Cruising is part of the American dream.

And cruise we did, with high tailfins that made us look like a school of sharks patrolling the boulevard. Actually, the tailfin was originally designed to make cars look like World War II fighter planes, the triangulated tips on a '56 Fairlane, '58 Fury or '59 Cadillac implying that it was aerodynamically sound and ready to leave the ground. We flew them to malt shops, to drive-in movies and to lovers' lane look-outs.

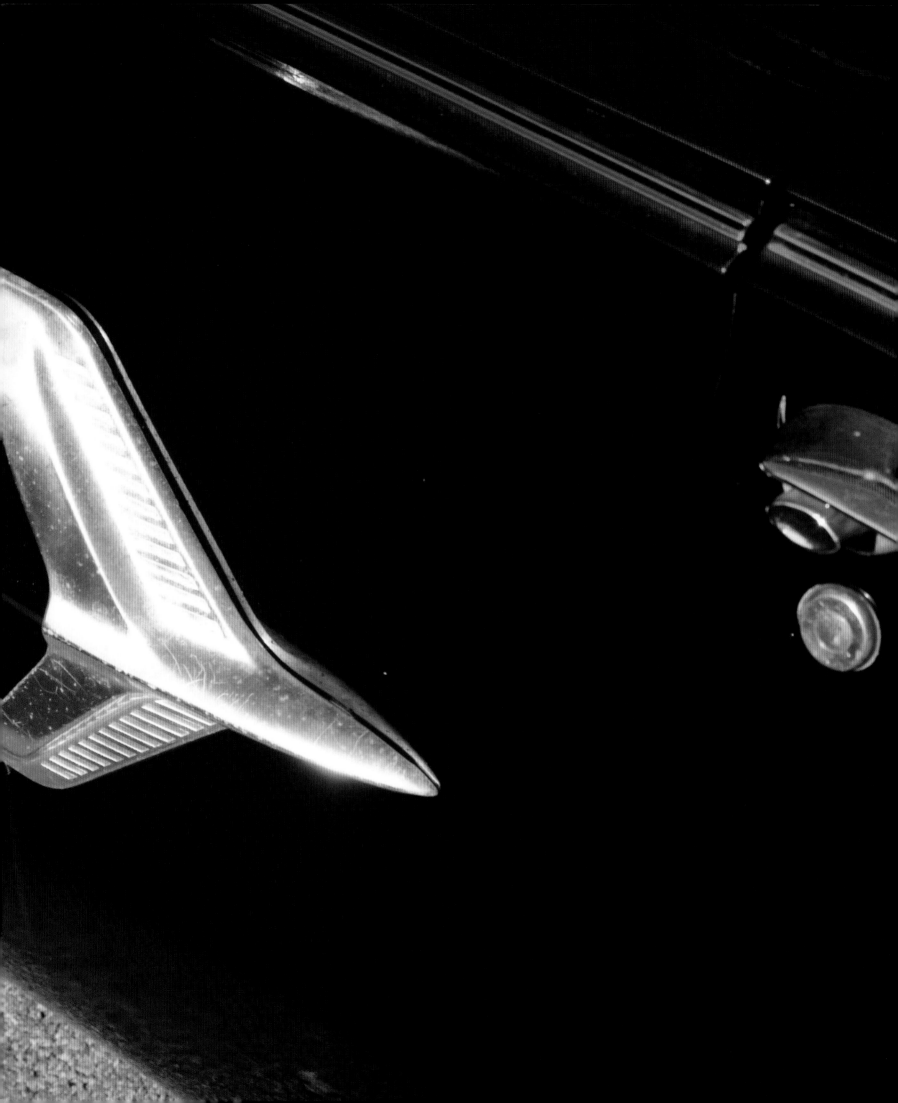

The right car was a ticket to Coolville, especially for young men. Hell, a guy didn't even have to be driving: With a heel propped on the fender and elbows on the trunk, you could pass for James Dean in the parking lot of a burger joint. Dean himself was a great lover of cars and represented the "live fast, die young" ethic that would, sadly, summarize his own life. An accomplished race-car driver, Dean was forbidden to race by a clause in his contract for the film *Giant*. But as soon as filming ended, he was back on the gas pedal of his Porsche 550 Spyder (nicknamed "Little Bastard"). On September 30th, 1955, Dean was on his way to a race in Palm Springs, California, with his mechanic, Rolf Weutherich, riding shotgun. An oncoming car crossed into Dean's lane on Highway 466 and hit him head-on. Weutherich was thrown clear but Dean, who was only twenty-four, was dead by the time they got him to a hospital.

Very few people drove boutique roadsters like Dean's Porsche, but we all

shared his taste for a car with sex appeal. If you look at the cars from prior decades, especially during World War II, they were all square and boxy. Early in the 1950s, American manufacturers like Chrysler, Ford and Chevrolet got a whiff of the emerging youth culture and fundamentally changed the direction of car design to match. Look at all that splashy chrome on a Plymouth Fury, the rounded corners on a T-Bird and the ruby-red tail lights on a Crown Victoria—cars looked like juke boxes, and juke boxes like cars. Rock 'n' roll sprang from these magic machines, and not just from the dashboard's radio. Cars shared the image and emotion of music. If you think about it, the same remains true some fifty years later: BMW's Mini Cooper has all the compact, bubble-shaped charm of an iPod. To this day, youth directs design.

Getting behind the wheel was never just a matter of traveling from point A to point B. Like the carmakers in Detroit banging together all that metal, rubber and leather, teenagers of the '50s and '60s looked through their windshields to the future.

THE WILLOWS

A seminal street corner group from Harlem, the Willows inspired many New York City doo wop acts who followed them. Their major hit, "Church Bells May Ring," featured chimes played on the recording by a then-unknown member of the Tokens, Neil Sedaka.

and worked them hard at the local radio stations, record stores and performance venues where they held sway. Lithe and eager indies like Jubilee, Scepter, Deluxe, Checker and Gee (one of the legendary doo wop labels owned by George Goldner), Chess, Vee-Jay, Specialty and Herald were able to negotiate narrow avenues of revenue that the bloated majors could not. They were also savvy enough not to let the majors swoop in and buy their artists' master recordings anymore. If a big label wanted to cash in on doo wop talent, they were going to pay through the nose first: Rather than hand over a hit, indies would position their entire company to be bought out by the corporate labels.

Sadly, even the most lucrative deals would still leave the talented artists with little more than lint in their pants pockets.

Singing Schoolboys

It would be too easy and too cynical to ascribe the success of doo wop to a plot dreamed up by the recording industry. Sure, the labels capitalized on a trend, then exploited its artists and inflated its exposure. But young people yearned for the music as an expression of their own identity. If the parents didn't like it, well, all the better. The idea that parents thought the music was sometimes silly, adolescent or shallow merely fueled the fire because then their children could possess the music as their own in a wave of self-righteous rebellion. Music simply provided the flashpoint for the perennial battle of the generations. doo wop, like its rock 'n' roll counterpoint, was a youth

THE SIX TEENS

Hailing from Los Angeles and equally divided between guys and gals, the Six Teens had no trouble finding their name: They were all teenagers, aged twelve to seventeen. Organized by member Ed Wells, who wrote their big hit, "A Casual Look," the Six Teens performed with acts like the Coasters—but only when they weren't hitting the books.

The Platters

MERCURY RECORDS

Mercury
70633X45
YW11548
Ram Music Inc.
(ASCAP) 2:33
Vocal
ONLY YOU (AND YOU ALONE)
(Buck Ram)
THE PLATTERS

music for every mood!

BROOK BENTON	THE PLATTERS	THE DIAMONDS
THE GAYLORDS	ERNESTINE ANDERSON	JAN AUGUST
DICK CONTINO	JOE MEDLIN	HERMAN CLEBANOFF
JIMMY PALMER	RICHARD HAYMAN	QUINCY JONES
JERRY MURAD'S HARMONICATS	MAX ROACH	PETE RUGOLO

MERCURY RECORD CORPORATION / CHICAGO, ILL. / established in 1947 on a sound basis!

Nothing less than vocal-group royalty, the Platters are among the most successful and most fondly remembered vocal artists of all time.

What imperiled all but a handful of doo wop groups was lack of professional support. But the Platters had Buck Ram. Buck not only had a law degree to back up his managerial skills, but had studied music and been an arranger for big bands like Tommy Dorsey, Count Basie and Duke Ellington. Suffice to say, the pipe-toting Buck had earned his credibility among musicians—and knew the ropes of the profession.

Buck saw great potential in the original Platters, four guys who had been earning their living as parking-lot attendants while roughing together their skills as a doo wop group. With a keen ear for pop potential, Buck became their vocal coach, manager and mentor. He also had the unique idea to add a female vocalist to the fold: Zola Taylor, who softened their vocal cushion and added a touch of grace to the Platters' stage presence. Finally, Buck quite literally orchestrated their success by writing and arranging some of the finest gems in doo wop history.

In July of 1955, the Platters—now a quintet with vocalist Tony Williams on lead—made their first run up the charts with "Only You." The song stayed on the charts for more than nine months, hitting #1 on the R&B charts, and #5 on the pop charts. Now, it was common at the time for white groups to cover songs by black artists and achieve bigger success with the borrowed tunes, and a white group called the Hilltoppers were covering "Only You." For the first time ever in rock 'n' roll, the black originators beat out the white cover band: The Platters topped the Hilltoppers.

The hits didn't stop after that, and the Platters followed for the next five years with more beauties from Buck's pen such as "The Great Pretender," "Twilight Time" and the serene "Smoke Gets in Your Eyes." They toured the world, had the first Top 10 LP by a rock 'n' roll group, and by the end of the fifties were international stars. In anyone else's hands, the vocalists would probably have been exploited down to their last dime as soon as the money started rolling in. However, Buck had made the wise decision to protect his artists. Having established The Five Platters, Inc. in 1956, each member of the group owned twenty percent of the corporate stock, and all received equal salaries. It was a rare move that ensured that each member was creatively—and financially—vested in the group.

The Platters could kick up a great mid-tempo melody, but they were balladeers by trade. Their liquid harmonies are more complex than just about any other band, with the possible exception of the Flamingos. But the complexity and perfection of the Flamingos is what kept that group out of the public eye. By contrast, one of the Platters' (and Buck's) brilliant strokes was to distill their talent into a very palatable style that anyone and everyone could enjoy. Without distancing themselves too far from a rhythm & blues foundation, they made music that was a little more "white." To my mind, they weren't pandering to white listeners but adapting some of the finest elements in R&B to the tastes of a broader audience.

They were sophisticated but didn't sound stuffy; they had pop sense but were never campy. They used simple lyrics and melodies, yet their songs were very skillfully honed. The Platters had a singular combination of soul, a tiny bit of gospel and a dizzying dose of romance that allowed them to cross barriers of race, age and gender. If you couldn't find something you liked in the Platters' catalog— take your choice of "Fools Fall in Love," "The Magic Touch" or "Harbor Lights"—you needed to be checked for a pulse.

The Platters had built a bridge between early vocal groups like the Mills Brothers and Ink Spots and the doo wop groups of the fifties. We didn't know it at the time, but they would also link the fifties to the future. Today, several different groups tour as one Platters combo or another, each laying claim to the name based on a single singer's membership. Some are valid, some strain the bounds of credibility, and most have spent as much time in litigation as they have on the big stage. Thankfully, the legal battles take place out of the spotlight while fans bask in the warm sound and sweet, romantic memories served up half a century ago by the Platters.

Vocal music crossed paths with rock 'n' roll rhythm, and fell in love. Vocal harmony plus rock 'n' roll equals doo wop.

movement—a shift in focus from one generation to the next. Adult resistance played right into the teenage mindset.

Nowhere was this more apparent than in the "schoolboy doo wop" that surfaced in 1956. Much of the doo wop already in circulation had been performed by groups in their late teens and early twenties, and now their little brothers wanted to play in the big boys' ballgame.

Made up of members as young as twelve and thirteen, the groups' high tenor leaders could easily be mistaken for girls, and their puppy-love lyrics belied their age. But for pre-teens feeling the very real aches and pains of a first love, the schoolboy bands provided a familiar voice they could recognize and trust. For the first time they heard songs about their own lives rather than more mature tales of one-night stands or relationships gone sour. Kids wanted to hear kids singing about kids.

Pioneered by Frankie Lymon and the Teenagers, the genre swelled with teeny-woppers like the Schoolboys ("Please Say You Want Me"), the Students ("I'm So Young"), the Teenchords ("Honey Honey," with Frankie's brother, Louis Lymon, singing lead) and the Tops ("Puppy Love"). It was Frankie Lymon, though, who was by far the best and brightest schoolboy star.

When they burst on the scene in early 1956 with "Why Do Fools Fall in Love," Frankie was a tender thirteen years old. (Grown-ups later chuckled when the story emerged that the boys had no experience of their own to draw on—they wrote the hit song after reading love poems penned by an adult neighbor's girlfriend.) Expressive and soulful far

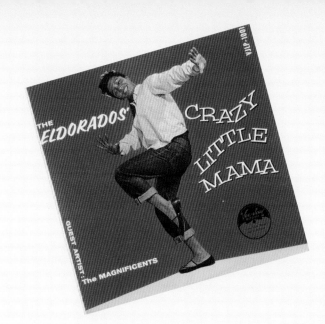

The Eldorados

Named for a sleek, sexy and expensive set of wheels, the El Dorados hailed from Chicago's South Side and were a prime example of doo wop, R&B and a little gospel thrown in. They had two back-to-back hits with "At My Front Door" and "I'll Be Forever Loving You."

The Sensations

Purveyors of the 1950s Philadelphia sound, the Sensations formed in 1954 and featured a female lead singer, Yvonne Mills. She later left to get married but was persuaded to reform the group in 1961 (as Mrs. Yvonne Baker) and scored their biggest hit "Let Me In."

The Davy Crockett Craze

Young people in the mid-1950s were looking for someone to believe in, and they could have done a lot worse than Davy Crockett. In the midst of the Cold War, he reminded us of American strength, justice and honor. Davy Crockett came to be a popular symbol of patriotism and heroism—even if we were getting all our facts from a few Walt Disney television specials.

The Crockett craze was one of the earliest multimedia happenings. It all kicked off with the three-part Disney series that began near the end of 1954. Soon the fabled frontiersman had captured the imaginations of American and British youth alike, and everybody started wearing coonskin caps like the Crockett character did. When "The Ballad of Davy Crockett" started running up the charts in 1955, it really fueled the excitement. Many artists eventually recorded the song, but the most memorable versions were the ones by Bill Hayes, who had the biggest hit with it in 1955, and the one by Fess Parker, since he starred as the dashing Davy in the TV specials. There were Davy Crockett books and comic books, Halloween outfits, lunch boxes, board games, even picture-card bubble gum! And of course, there was a crazy coonskin cap on everybody's head. For a kid, putting on that cap was a chance to feel like an American hero of the old West.

There was no downside to Crockett—his story was understood to carry an all-positive, all-American message—and the craze crossed the generation gap. If you lived in the '50s, you just can't read these words without hearing the melody and imagining Fess Parker in his cap and fringe jacket, with his trusty rifle in hand:

Davy, Davy Crockett
King of the wild frontier!

FESS PARKER

The world might never have heard Michael Jackson fronting the Jackson 5 had Michael not studied every note and nuance sung by little Frankie Lymon.

beyond his years, the young singer wowed audiences twice and three times his age while becoming the first teen idol of doo wop—and arguably the first African American teen idol ever.

Older listeners may only have been enjoying the high-flying tones of Frankie's castrato-like vocals. To his baby-faced contemporaries, however, Frankie was plucking their heartstrings, even with lyrics like *I promise to remember the meaning of romance* and the lessons he taught fellow pupils in "The ABC's of Love." These kids were talented, but how could they know the meaning of love? Their parents were still trying to figure it out!

The Teenagers exemplified the schoolboy scene but also proved to be one of the most influential acts in all of doo wop. They've even been credited for inspiring the production values of Berry Gordy's Motown label. The world might never have heard Michael Jackson fronting the Jackson 5 had Michael not studied every note and nuance sung by little Frankie Lymon.

THE SCHOOLBOYS

Barely out of grade school, this Harlem-based band of juveniles personified the trend of children singing to children. Though their song themes—the highs and lows of young love—were typical for the day, in their case puppy love was probably more accurate. They did score a hit with "Shirley" in 1957.

Don Julian and the Meadowlarks

This quartet of soft balladeers from the City of Angels were still in high school when they signed with Dootone records. Their first release for the label, "Heaven and Paradise," was a moderate hit.

TEEN FLICKS

SAL MINEO, JAMES DEAN AND COREY ALLEN IN REBEL WITHO

Radio's Alan Freed had national recognition by 1956, and sometimes he put his notoriety to great use. But then we had his rock 'n' roll movies. There was a whole string of them for about three years: *Rock Around the Clock* (1956), *Rock, Rock, Rock* (1956), *Mr. Rock and Roll* (1957), *Don't Knock the Rock* (1957) and *Go, Johnny Go!* (1959). If I had to put my own rating on them, I would rate them G . That's G as in "Gee, do we really have to watch this awful thing?" The plots were really laughable, when they bothered with a plot line at all. For the musical acts in them, though, these movies provided a rare opportunity to be seen and heard by an international audience. Inevitably, the big climax scene is a rock 'n' roll dance, providing a showcase for a barrage of bands including the Platters, Frankie Lymon and the Teenagers, the Flamingos and the Moonglows, as well straight-up rock and rollers like Bill Haley, Chuck Berry and Little Richard.

When Hollywood trained its spotlight on rock 'n' roll, it

In both rock 'n' roll and R&B, the artists were distracted by the lure of the silver screen as they were courted by the producers and directors of these films. At least we got a few good soundtracks out of them.

The rock 'n' roll movies were aimed at a young audience but a whole different class of "teen angst" movies had already captured the teenage experience in a truer and more compelling way. First there was Marlon Brando as the untameable biker in 1953's *The Wild One*, which made the life of an outlaw look enticing. James Dean represented the depth and difficulty of misunderstood youth in his two 1955 films, *Giant* and *Rebel Without a Cause*. That same year, *Blackboard Jungle* featured a classroom full of rebels, offering an unsettling account of what happens when the inmates (kids) run the asylum (school). That movie also featured the song "Rock Around the Clock" in the opening credits, ensuring that teenage movie-goers would immediately be enraptured. Those few minutes of movie music kick-started the age—and

Teenagers swing
to the beat in
1956's `Rock,
Rock, Rock´

GENE VINCENT AND THE BLUE CAPS

An early rock 'n' roll "rebel," Gene Vincent entered the music business after leaving the navy, where he had severely damaged one of his legs in a motorcycle accident. Expertly blending rockabilly with doo wop, Vincent and his Blue Caps (who really did wear blue caps) scored big with "Be-Bop'A'Lula" in 1956.

Lee Andrews and the Hearts

Philadelphia is sometimes called the "sister city" of New York, and the southward sibling is a little warmer and a little less rough around the edges. The same can be said for the wonderful Lee Andrews and the Hearts, who hailed from the City of Brotherly Love and spread a lot of it around.

Timeless songs like "Teardrops," "Bells of St. Mary's" and "White Cliffs of Dover" have the energy and streetwise sense of the inner city, but there's also a purity and simplicity to them. The group never sounded over-produced or as if they were over-reaching. Lee Andrews and the Hearts fused gospel and R&B music in a way the two hadn't been paired before, and they set the stage for the Philly Soul groups who would follow in the '60s.

As great as they were, though, the group never hit the big big time. Clearly, the quality was there in tunes like "Long Lonely Nights" and "Bluebirds of Happiness," but they were dogged by competing covers and exploitative business practices. Their down-tempo, mellow sound lacked the audience it deserved.

Sometimes it seems like there's a jukebox in my mind, and all these great doo wop records keep playing back again and again. Everyone has their favorite numbers to punch and their favorite artists to hear. I decided on Lee Andrews and the Hearts long ago.

Common Denominators

Even with its youngest members just graduating grade school, doo wop music was all grown up by the mid-1950s. When you consider the hundreds—literally—of doo wop groups that came down the pike in the ensuing years, it's amazing how many common denominators they shared. Looking back, we can see that the defining characteristics were in place by 1956.

Beyond the quality of their harmonies, the dominance of four- and five-man groups, and bass vocalists who could sing *dip dip dip* and *yip yip yip* at wall-shaking frequencies, the similarities were uncanny. For those keeping score at home, here are ten parts to the profile.

1. Family members Brothers, sisters and cousins formed the nucleus of countless doo wop groups, and they were often shepherded to success by parents, aunts and uncles.

2. Schoolyard singing Bands were rounded out by friends from school. Many jump-started their careers after performing in talent shows and being encouraged by a teacher.

3. Roots in the church Gospel and spiritual music formed the soul of doo wop, and the first experience of young vocalists was often singing on Sundays.

4. No formal music education They learned from one another and from musically inclined members of their family, their church, and their community.

By 1955, the whole equation of vocal music had changed. The previous generation of pop audiences listened to lyrics and a melody; the new generation wanted to feel a beat.

> *Industry coffers were brimming with cash from record receipts, but little of the overflow ever made it downstream to the artists.*

5. Playing checkers with personnel Doo wop's family tree is a tangle of criss-crossing branches. Sustaining a fixed line-up, even over a short career, was a rarity (Little Anthony and the Imperials being an exception to the rule).

6. Label jumping Whether or not a group wanted to stick with the record company that signed them, the labels were seldom loyal. The Hollywood Flames probably hold the record, having recorded for nineteen labels.

7. Label exploitation Part and parcel of doo wop business was that the groups made millions for record companies while securing just a fraction of the money for themselves.

8. Anonymity The vast majority of doo wop singers were faceless to the audiences who loved their music. Their best bet for standing out visually was to don a shiny suit or choose a gimmick like wearing turbans (the Turbans) or "marcelling" their hair (the Marcels). Ben E. King, Clyde McPhatter and Frankie Lymon are rare exceptions to the rule.

9. One-hit wonders In all of pop music, no style features more bands identified with a single song each.

10. City boys America's heartland may have loved doo wop music, but it didn't contribute to the talent pool. A few chart-toppers hailed from cities in California (Robins, Platters, Coasters) and Illinois (Flamingos, Dells, Spaniels), but East Coast urban areas were doo wop's domain—none more so than New York City.

THE COLTS

A classic one-hit wonder, the Colts met in the halls of Los Angeles City College and released their song "Adorable" written by Buck Ram, manager of the Platters. Though a few weeks ahead of the Drifters' cover version, The Colts were no match for the superstar group, who stopped them at the gate.

THE VALENTINES

Remembered now for their warm vocal harmonies, the New York-based Valentines never had a hit climb the national charts. One 1955 song, "Lilly Maebelle," became a DJ favorite, allowing them to score gigs at Alan Freed shows and more, but they eventually disbanded in 1958.

The T-Bird vs. the Edsel

The 1950s were the golden age of the American automobile, we wanted to do our cruising in style, and U.S. automakers—with their seemingly endless variations of big-finned, streamlined designs—were ready to oblige. One of these cars, the Ford Thunderbird, lovingly called the T-Bird, is one of the most iconic, beloved classic cars ever made. Another, the Edsel, also manufactured by Ford, is remembered as one of the most spectacular disappointments in the history of the industry.

From the day the first T-Bird went on the market in 1955, it seemed like everybody—girls, guys and parents—wanted one. With its high-powered V-8 engine, distinctive "porthole" roof-side windows and removable top, the T-Bird was a car that said fun, fun, fun. To guys, it was the perfect machine to show off to your girlfriend. The driver and passenger seats being so close together didn't hurt either—it was the perfect make-out vehicle. More versions of the car would be produced over the years, but back in the '50s the sleek, sporty T-Bird was the stuff dreams were made of.

The Edsel, on the other hand, turned out to be the stuff of nightmares, especially for Ford's dealers and executives. With its characteristic (many said ugly) "horsecollar" grille, the Edsel was introduced to the public with an infamously drawn-out ad campaign and a one-hour special on national TV.

A strong recession, plus the fact that the Edsel was greatly overpriced when compared with the other "mid-range" cars it was competing against (and unlike ad promises, nothing new), spelled its early demise. The company ceased production in 1960, after only three years. Ever since, the word Edsel has been synonymous with "marketing disaster."

Though one was labeled a dream car and one a commercial flop, today both the T-Bird and the Edsel sell for sky-high prices on the collectors' market.

CREATURE FROM THE BLACK LAGOON

Starring

RICHARD CARLSON · JULIA ADAMS

with RICHARD DENNING · ANTONIO MORENO · NESTOR PAIVA · WHIT BISSELL

SCI-FI AND HORROR MOVIES: ALIENS, MONSTERS AND MAYHEM

Once it was human... even as you and I!

SHE HAD TO KILL THE THING HER HUSBAND HAD BECOME—

BUT COULD SHE?

The Fly

IN CINEMASCOPE AND TERROR-COLOR BY DE LUXE

THE MONSTER CREATED BY ATOMS GONE WILD!

FOR YOUR OWN GOOD WE URGE YOU NOT TO SEE IT ALONE!

AL HEDISON · PATRICIA OWENS · VINCENT PRICE · HERBERT MARSHALL

Produced and Directed by KURT NEUMANN · Screen Play by JAMES CLAVELL

Science fiction movies had their heyday in the 1950s, and rightly so. We had a Cold War brewing and the threat of "invasion" was considered very real. With art being a reliable barometer of social concerns, films like *Invasion of the Body Snatchers* and *War of the Worlds* played on our paranoia, substituting

Frankie Lymon
AND THE TEENAGERS

"Kid music" or "schoolboy sound" was the tag first assigned to Frankie Lymon and the Teenagers. Tough to argue against it, too, with a pre-pubescent Frankie out front singing naïve ideas about love in his thirteen-year-old tenor. But when "Why Do Fools Fall in Love" shot to the top of the charts in 1956, it was clear that this group of New York City youngsters was serving up more than kid stuff. It was immediately taken seriously enough that three competing covers of the same song shot across the Teenagers' bow—but they were sailing to success by then, and the original version catapulted them to international renown.

Frankie and the Teenagers were together for just a year and a half—a remarkably short period, considering the long reach of their influence. In that time they heated up the charts on both sides of the Atlantic with hits like "I Want You to Be My Girl," "The ABC's of Love," and "I'm Not a Juvenile Delinquent," a favorite in England.

Just when it looked like a long and prosperous future was spread out before them, the group split. Frankie went one way and the Teenagers the other in 1957, and neither would recapture the success they'd enjoyed together.

A short-lived career was characteristic of doo wop acts, the saving grace being that so many of them reunited years later to relive the music they'd made together. Sadly, the Teenagers and Frankie had only one opportunity, in 1965, to relive their musical moments. Frankie died of a drug overdose in 1968. He was just twenty-five years old.

The group's sound is said to have had a major impact on early productions by Berry Gordy Jr. at his Motown label. Had Frankie and friends not forged the path they did, Gordy may never have believed that youngsters like the Jackson Five or "Little Stevie" Wonder could sell records. Stevie, Michael, Diana Ross, the Temptations and countless other artists may never even have been moved to make their music without young Frankie Lymon's inspiration.

Classics such as 'Forbidden Planet' and 'The Day the Earth Stood Still' asked us to look a little deeper inside ourselves.

LOCK MARTIN (AS GORT) AND MICHAEL RENNIE AS KLAATU IN THE DAY THE EARTH STOOD STILL

GEON (AS DR. MORBIUS) AND ROBBY THE ROBOT IN FORBIDDEN PLANET

aliens for the threat of communism. Audiences loved the campy thrills and chills of *The Blob* and *The Creature from the Black Lagoon*, but it wasn't all brainless escapism. Classics such as *The Day the Earth Stood Still* and *Forbidden Planet* asked us to look a little deeper inside ourselves, while *The Thing* set a standard for thrillers to come. Though good always triumphed in the end, it wasn't without sacrifice and lessons learned. These movies can't compare to the special effects of today's fantasy films, but they were entertaining and conveyed a simple, clear message: There was hope for the future. We needed to believe that then, and still do.

Meanwhile, horror movies like *The Fly* reworked a threat as old as Frankenstein: Don't mess with Mother Nature, no matter how good your intentions. Like mad scientists, the struggle between good and evil is a horror film staple. However, this was also the decade of radiation-infused mutant monsters and humans (*Them*, *Tarantula*, *The Amazing Colossal Man*) destroying all in their path before they too are destroyed. A nod to the horrors of nuclear warfare, these films preached the perceived mixed blessings of science and progress.

SCI-FI AND HORROR MOVIES: ALIENS, MONSTERS AND MAYHEM

Once it was human... even as you and I!

SHE HAD TO KILL THE THING HER HUSBAND HAD BECOME—

BUT COULD SHE?

The Fly

IN CINEMASCOPE AND TERROR-COLOR BY DE LUXE

THE MONSTER CREATED BY ATOMS GONE WILD!

FOR YOUR OWN GOOD WE URGE YOU NOT TO SEE IT ALONE!

KURT NEUMANN · JAMES CLAVELL

AL HEDISON · PATRICIA OWENS · VINCENT PRICE · HERBERT MARSHALL

Science fiction movies had their heyday in the 1950s, and rightly so. We had a Cold War brewing and the threat of "invasion" was considered very real. With art being a reliable barometer of social concerns, films like *Invasion of the Body Snatchers* and *War of the Worlds* played on our paranoia, substituting

JAMES WHITMORE IN THEM

The Cleftones

Herbie Cox, lead tenor of the Cleftones, is a sweetheart of a guy. He's always smiling and full of life. Herbie had a hand in writing a lot of the Cleftones' music, and one reason their songs are so infectious is that they mirror his personality and charm.

The Cleftones were all buddies from Jamaica High School in Queens, New York. Herbie and two friends had a group called the Clefs, and they joined forces with another two fellas in a group called the Silvertones. Legend has it that they got their start singing campaign slogans for a school election. We don't know if their party won the vote, but we do know the Cleftones won over audiences from the very start.

Taking a shot at success beyond the schoolroom, the teenagers secured an audition with George Goldner, who in 1955 was running the Rama label from a building in midtown Manhattan. The boys sang half an hour's worth of tunes right there in Goldner's office, and by the time they left, they were booked to record. The first single they released, "You Baby You," was the first song released on Goldner's new Gee label, marking an auspicious start to a record company that would be front and center in doo wop history.

Catchy classics like "Can't We Be Sweethearts" and "Little Girl Of Mine" helped the Cleftones etch their own place in history. Later in life, Herbie's personality and smarts sent him up through the ranks of big business. True to his heart and his art, though, he stayed involved with doo wop. Herbie went on to manage the Chordettes ("Mr. Sandman," "Lollipop"), and still sings with a modern-day incarnation of the Cleftones.

The Turbans

Standing out from the crowd was a challenge for many doo wop groups, the vast majority of whom were well-dressed quartets or quintets of men ooh'ing and ahh'ing behind microphones while dancing a short step in unison. On the busy East Coast scene, Philadelphia's own Turbans were already distinguished by the crisp falsetto of young Al Banks, but their manager sought another level of differentiation. According to Banks, their manager suggested they emulate crosstown contemporaries the Red Caps (not to be confused with the Five Red Caps, who were from Los Angeles), but bassist Charlie Williams retorted that he'd sooner be seen in a turban than a cap. Sometimes you have to be careful about your ultimatums.

Aside from silly headwear, the Turbans are remembered for 1955's "When You Dance." That was the first time the masses heard the words *doo wop* clearly sung in a song. Ask ten doo wop aficionados who actually coined the term and you may get ten different answers: A small-time L.A. group called the Dundees had sung the same syllables in 1954, but few people ever heard their records; the words can be heard in a 1953 recording by the Drifters/Clyde McPhatter called "Let the Boogie Woogie Roll," but that song wasn't released until 1960. Doo wop didn't take its name for many years after the genre's glory days, so the truth remains a mystery of history. But "When You Dance" was the first Top 40 hit containing the phrase, which makes a strong case for the Turbans.

THE RAINBOWS

A teen group from Washington, D.C., the Rainbows attracted a roster of members that included future solo stars such as Marvin Gaye, Don Covay and Billy Stewart. In 1955 they signed with Red Robin records and hit with "Mary Lee" and "They Say."

THE TEEN QUEENS

Two sisters from Los Angeles, the Teen Queens recorded "Eddie My Love" written by their brother. Another teen age soap opera set to music, "Eddie My Love" remains a doo wop staple.

The Heartbeats

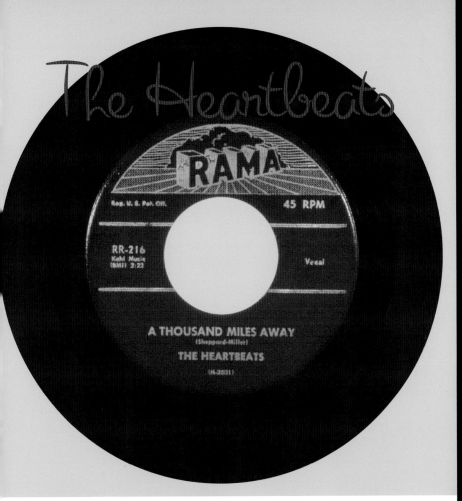

RAMA
Reg. U. S. Pat. Off.
45 RPM

RR-216
Kahl Music
(BMI) 2:22
Vocal

A THOUSAND MILES AWAY
(Sheppard-Miller)

THE HEARTBEATS

(H-2021)

W hen lead singer James "Shep" Sheppard penned his heartfelt lament, "A Thousand Miles Away," to a girlfriend who had recently moved, it brought national attention to this tight-knit group from Jamaica, Queens. He later formed Shep and the Limelites in 1961 and scored a hit with "Daddy's Home," a tender tune about returning home from war.

The Four Fellows

A smooth quartet from Brooklyn, their big hit was "Soldier Boy," written by member David Jones while serving in Korea. Not to be confused with the Shirelles classic of the same name, "Soldier Boy" stayed on the charts for several months. Shortly afterwards, Jones left to join the Rays.

MARLON BRANDO (AS JOHNNY) AND YVONNE DOUGHTY (AS BRITCHES) IN THE WILD ONE

FASHIONS OF THE FIFTIES

Leather jackets, tee shirts, poodle skirts and saddle shoes—those were fashions! As soon as Brando swaggered across movie screens in his leather jacket, a new look was born. Each generation defines itself through its music and clothes, but the teenagers of the 1950s broke the mold. Guys poured on the pomade and created gravity-defying hairstyles while the gals buzzed in their beehives. Form-fitting pants and stiletto pumps added a nice, sexy edge while dungarees with rivets (also known as blue jeans) moved from work clothes to everyday wear.

SAL MINEO

THE COASTERS WITH DICK CLARK

The Scene, the Sound, and the Glory

Well, well, well—good evening, everybody! We're comin' at you live from the stage of our rockin', hoppin' dance party, and boy do we have a wonderful bunch of people here tonight! So get your dancin' shoes on, 'cause you don't have to be in the hall to have a ball! Enough talkin'—let's get rockin'! Here's another jet-propelled recording that rocketed right up to the Top 25. It's Dion and the Belmonts with "I Wonder Why"…

With little more than a bandstand and a dance floor, any space could become the scene of a rock 'n' roll party. Armories, state fairgrounds, municipal rooms and church basements were all converted into dance halls, and fast-talking deejays inspired audiences from the stage like they were preaching to a congregation. On Saturday nights in the late '50s, young hearts were *thump-thump-thumping* to the beat of rock 'n' roll.

Doo wop stars great and small were enjoying time in the spotlight right alongside their rock 'n' roll brothers. Young crowds flocked to shows and danced the night away when the groups they'd heard on the radio came to town. Just a single hit on the charts was enough to justify a bus tour, so promoters really had to load up a bill if the audience was going to hear an evening full of familiar music. It wasn't uncommon to find five or six bands sharing the stage on a single night. There was enough music to go around but rarely enough from any one act, so performers would

Music had become more than just something to listen to; it was now something to move to.

also cover one another's hits to round out a set. The kids were lenient listeners, though, and most of the time they didn't even know the difference. They were too busy having fun.

American Bandstand premiered on ABC television in 1957, and while it was a first for TV, dance parties had already become a focal point for teenage entertainment. One-hit wonders and local talent ruled the small stages while headliners like Dion and the Belmonts or the Drifters could draw a big crowd to a major concert-hall venue. The bill would be backfilled by smaller acts and hosted by "boss jocks" like Alan Freed, Murray the K, Buddy Dean (Baltimore), Hal Jackson (New York), Porky "The Daddy-o of Radio" Chedwick (Pittsburgh), Dick Biondi, "The Wild I-Tralian" and Jerry "the Geator with the Heater" Blavat (Philadelphia), who whipped youngsters into a frenzy when they announced their favorite groups or thrilled a concert-goer with the chance to request a song into the microphone.

Music had become more than just something to listen to; it was something to move to. Songs with a beat were like physical therapy for the teenaged set, who got off their duffs to shake out their stress, their frustration and their fears. The mellow, mature side of vocal music was clearly out of fashion; doo wop did best when it rubbed shoulders with rock 'n' roll.

"Hey, you got your rock 'n' roll in my doo wop!"

Rock 'n' roll had an absolute latch on doo wop in the late '50s. The two styles had melded, fusing their attitudes as well as their sounds. People wanted to hear sound and feel rhythm, and doo wop delivered in countless shake-a-leg hits like

SUPER ATTRACTIONS
presents

The BIGGEST SHOW OF STARS FOR '57

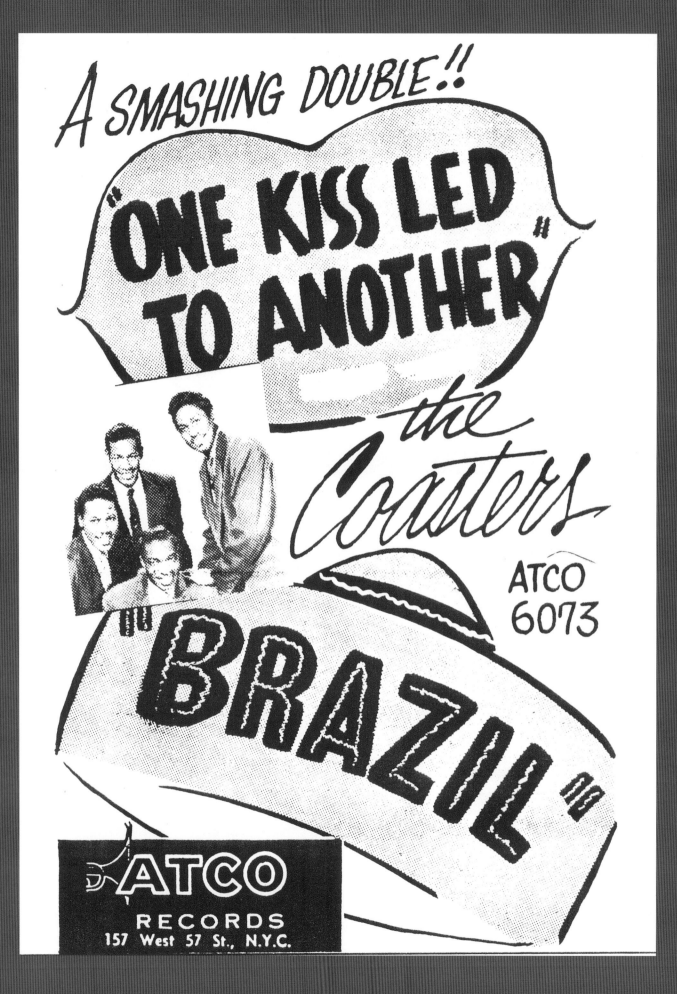

The Coasters

The Coasters took a very different path to success than most doo wop groups did. For starters, their path began on the West Coast, and that's the origin of their name, despite the roller coasters pictured on a handful of album covers. Setting them even further apart was the content and delivery of their hits. While all the other guys were singing tunes to worship and woo the women, the Coasters were going for a laugh. You might say the Coasters were like the class clowns of Doo wop High.

Like many great comics, not to mention many doo wop artists, the Coasters' best material was written with someone else's pen. Jerry Lieber and Mike Stoller, a musical tour de force, wrote the group's chart-topping hits and were fundamentally responsible for putting the Coasters together in the first place. The pair had their own label, Spark Records, and had steered the L.A.-based group the Robins to success. When Atlantic Records wanted to move the group back East, two of the Robins refused to leave the nest. Lead tenor Carl Gardner and bass man Bobby Nunn stayed in L.A. and formed the Coasters. Instead of having to split their bet between the two bands, Lieber and Stoller doubled down. In time they would cash out on both coasts.

Teenagers loved the Coasters' playful delivery and were overjoyed to hear someone singin' their proverbial song when the lyrics honed in on teen angst. "Yakety Yak" was like an anthem for them as they squirmed under controlling parents who demanded they *Take out the papers and the trash / or you don't get no spending cash*. On "Charlie Brown," pubescent males could only hope their voices would deepen enough to sing the booming bass hook, *Why's everybody always pickin' on me?*

The Coasters weren't entirely about yaks and yuks, but they did laugh their way into our hearts. In 1987, the Coasters become the first vocal group to be inducted in the Rock and Roll Hall of Fame.

Dion and the Belmonts

ion and the Belmonts represented some of the best doo wop New York City ever had to offer. That's saying something, too, not only because NYC was doo wop central but because in a music dominated by black singers, these were Italians straight off the streets—in fact, they took their name from Belmont Avenue in the Bronx—and within their first year went straight up the charts.

A clear measure of success for doo wop groups was crossing over to a white audience. Dion and the boys were among a handful of white doo wop acts who contributed so significantly by reversing the equation: They hand-held white audiences and led them to "black music." Great performances on classics like "I Wonder Why," "Teenager in Love," and their version of Cole Porter's "In the Still of the

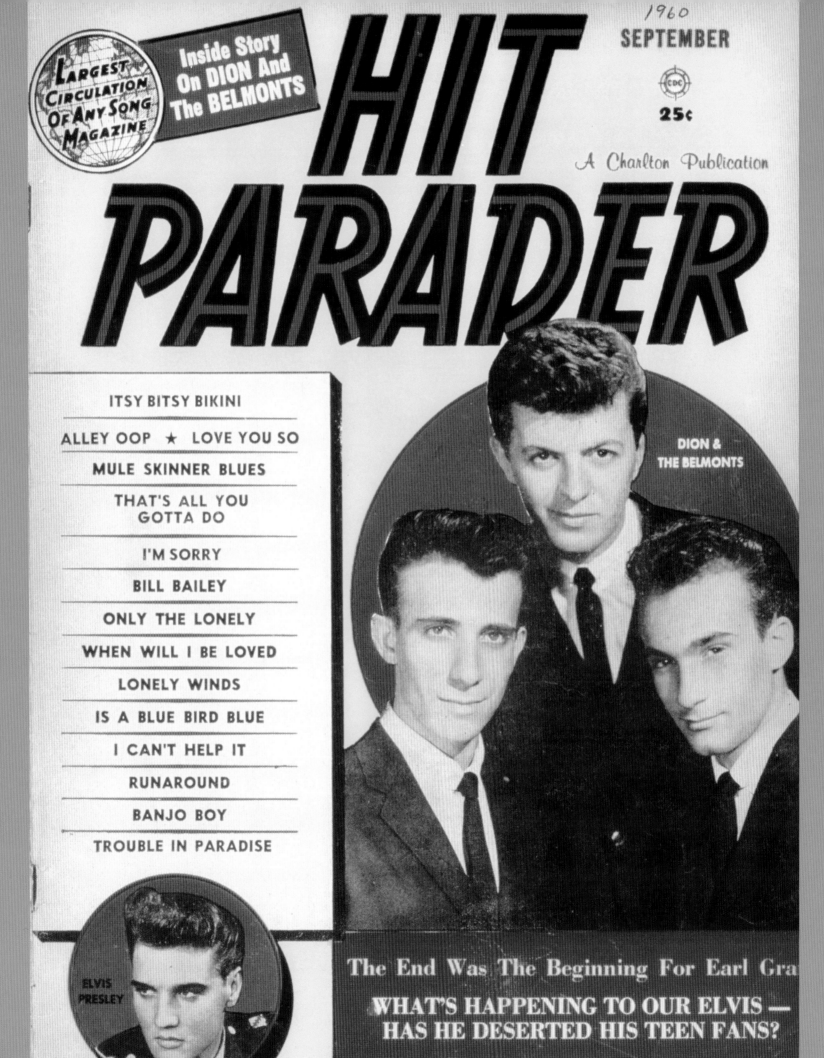

Night" (which has the same title but is not the same song as the Five Satins' classic) earned them respect on both sides of the fence. They were the first white act ever to be booked into Harlem's famed Apollo Theater.

The conclusion of the 1950s was an endpoint for Dion and the Belmonts in a few very significant ways. In February of 1959, the group had been out on the Winter Dance Party tour that ended so tragically with the passing of tourmates Buddy Holly, Ritchie Valens and the Big Bopper (see The Day the Music Died). In 1960, the Belmonts and Dion split. The Belmonts continued, to mixed commercial success, while Dion adopted the Del-Satins as his backup band and starting to cut the rock 'n' roll edge a little harder. He had enormous hits as a solo artist like "Runaround Sue," "The Wanderer" and, in 1968, the aching "Abraham, Martin and John." If you look closely enough, you can find Dion on the cover of the Beatles' Sgt. Pepper's Lonely Hearts Club Band.

New York still loves Dion and the Belmonts, so much so that they honored them with a "Dion and the Belmonts Way" Avenue.

THE FALCONS

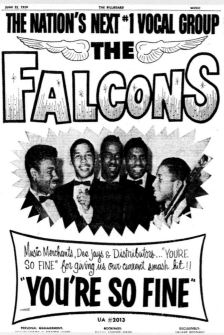

The Falcons had a major hit with "You're So Fine" in '59. Originally released on Flick Records, the song probably would have disappeared if the small label hadn't recognized its own limitations. Flick flipped the song to a powerful United Artist label, who had the money, marketing and merchandising to give the song its due.

The group may not be a household name, but they're not short on bragging rights. The Falcons' sound was drenched in soul and gospel—"You're So Fine" featured the vocals of Joe Stubbs and is sometimes marked as the first real soul record. They would reconfirm their place at the soul-music starting gate in 1962 with the release of "I Found a Love," sung by a fierce young Falcon named Wilson Pickett.

the Shells' "Baby Oh Baby," the Falcons' "You're So Fine" and the Del-Vikings' "Come Go With Me."

Vocal music had once been known for its refined orchestrations of a cappella harmonies, but this classic era of doo wop concentrated on the fun stuff: a topping of candy-coated falsetto, middle voices singing words you couldn't find in any dictionary and a bottom end that rattled and rolled. It was that low range, especially, that made us want to move. If you ask the bass guitar player of a rock 'n' roll band where he finds the beat, he'll tell you he locks to the bass drum. In the same way, it's the bass singers in doo wop groups who are most closely tied into the rhythm, and that's why they were such a hit with young listeners. Their bass lines tapped the primitive rhythm that exists in all of us (we're back to the cave, people!). Even among the mildest and meekest, a bass rhythm awakens our drive.

Plus, the bass singers held the coolest job in music while guaranteeing a good time. Just think of the booming bass in "Who's That Knockin'" by the Genies or "Yakety Yak" by the Coasters. And everybody in the civilized world knows that great *yip-yip-yip* hook in the Silhouettes' "Get a Job."

Doo wop was easy to listen to, easy to follow and easy to sing along to—all key factors in the success of any popular sound. Here in its heyday, doo wop was developing both artistically and professionally, yet it hadn't become overly sophisticated in either sense. The groups didn't feel a need to be especially progressive in their writing or arranging, and they weren't heavily pressured by the record labels to deliver more "product." That was the beauty of it, really. If the music had become too complicated or

Vocal music had once been known for its refined orchestrations of a cappella harmonies, but this classic era of doo wop concentrated on the fun stuff.

*Best Wishes
The
Jaguars*

The Jaguars

The Jaguars met at Fremont High School in Los Angeles and were an early interracial group known for smooth "make out music" like "The Way You Look Tonight." There must have been something in the curriculum at Fremont because it also spawned the Meadowlarks, the Hollywood Flames and the Medallions.

NORMAN FOX AND THE ROB-ROYS

The Rob-Roys were a groundbreaking doo wop group, not so much for the quality of their songs, but because they were an early example of an interracial group. Hailing from the Bronx, the Rob-Roys named themselves after the popular drink, and enjoyed a modest hit with "Tell Me Why," followed up with extra cheese for "Pizza Pie."

The Danleers

A smooth-sounding quintet from Brooklyn, New York, the Danleers recorded a classic, "One Summer Night." Written by their manager, "One Summer Night" is considered a quintessential summer rock anthem, enjoyed to this day.

The Aquatones

A one-hit wonder from Valley Stream, Long Island, the Aquatones were discovered at a local talent show. Their chart climber "You," released in 1958, was written by lead singer Larry Vannata.

The Tune Weavers

Originally from Boston, the Tone Weavers became the Tune Weavers when a local announcer mispronounced their name. However, they will remain a doo wop fixture and birthday staple with their 1957 hit "Happy Happy Birthday Baby."

manipulated, it would have lost its folksiness. By virtue of doo wop's pure simplicity, it had enduring charm.

Heroes of the day

One of the curiosities of doo wop is that the music was known to millions at its peak while the artists themselves were known to none. Nearly to the last man, doo wop singers were faceless. Just take a look at the images in these pages and you'll see there's not a lot of variation in the suits, the poses, the hairdos, or the lineups of quartets and quintets. Without the captions, how many groups could be named, even by a connoisseur? Teens who could sing every syllable of "In the Still of the Night" wouldn't know the Five Satins if they had walked into the room. But if Bobby Darin walked in, girls would faint, ice-cream sodas would spill and jaws would drop.

For better or for worse, no marketing or merchandising surrounded doo wop singers. Perhaps the record industry didn't perceive that they had anything to sell with a group of four or five black singers, but aside from a few novelty tunes (for example, "Western Movies" by the Olympics, "Ling, Ting, Tong" by the Charms and by the Five Keys, "Charlie Brown" by the Coasters) the style was unencumbered by marketing ploys. When a leader stuck out from the crowd—like a Frankie Lymon, a Sam Cooke or a Clyde McPhatter—marketers had a little more to hold on to, but even those artists were rarely recognized unless they went on to solo success. This was a style built on groups, not individuals. doo wop was a team sport.

PARAGONS

The Paragons' big claim to fame is a Winley 'battle-of-the-bands' top-selling LP, 'The Paragons meet the Jesters'

A Brooklyn street corner group, the Paragons are for those who really love doo wop. They had a hit with "Florence" and were part of the Winley Records group of doo wop acts that included the Jesters. The Paragons' big claim to fame is a Winley "battle of the bands" top selling LP, "The Paragons meet the Jesters." Released in 1959, it was like a doo wop version of the Sharks and the Jets, with the track listing alternating between Brooklyn's Paragons and Harlem's Jesters. It's a great collection, but it's also one of the compilation records thsat inadvertently turned doo wop into nostalgic music before its time was over.

The Shirelles

Anyone with an AM radio and a heart had a soft spot for the Shirelles. These four high-school pals from Passaic, New Jersey, were as sweet as the songs they floated over the airwaves in the late '50s and '60s.

It all started as good, clean fun. In 1957, a teacher heard the girls harmonizing in the gym at Passaic High and suggested they try their luck in the school talent show. They wrote a teenaged girl's song of week-long love just for that performance and brought down the house with "I Met Him on a Sunday." When a friend offered to introduce them to her mother, who owned a small record label, the foursome initially laughed it off. But in February of 1958 they conceded, recording two songs that would soon be picked up by Decca Records. By April, their talent-show composition charted #49 in Billboard.

The Shirelles went on to become the most popular girl group of the early '60s and were the first to override all the obstacles facing performers who were both black and female. In fact, they almost missed out on their first #1 hit because they were reluctant to record a song they thought sounded too "white." A little-known Brooklyn songwriter named Carole King and co-writer Gerry Goffin had penned a song called "Tomorrow." By the time the girls accepted the song and made it their own, it had become "Will You Love Me Tomorrow." With Carole King on drums, it topped the U.S. charts late in 1960 and garnered international attention

for the group. (King recorded her own version a decade later on her album Tapestry. And Dionne Warwick, who had subbed in the Shirelles, had the girls sing backup when she recorded the song in 1983.)

They went on to have so many huge hits: "Baby It's You," "Mama Said," "Boys"…the list goes on and on. They were loved by everyone. The Beatles even said that the Shirelles were their favorite American group, and they recorded both "Boys" and "Baby It's You." There were many great renditions of Shirelles songs, but I always preferred that very natural sound the girls had themselves.

Their second #1 smash was "Soldier Boy," in 1962. I remember right around that time being asked to entertain the troops at Fort Dix in New Jersey. I was just starting out in radio, and I didn't know too many people. But I loved the Shirelles, so I called Shirley Alston (aka Shirley Owens) and asked if they'd come perform with me. Right there on the phone she said, "Sure! We'd be very happy to entertain the troops with you." I picked them up on a bus I had hired, and we all went down to Fort Dix. They sang "Soldier Boy" and all their hits—they were fabulous, and the boys in uniform loved them. They spent so much time meeting the guys and talking to everyone. The Shirelles held their fans in high esteem.

The soldiers went crazy for them that day at Fort Dix. Not in a sensual way, but in a sweet way. I think it's because the girls reminded them of home. They were local girls, but they belonged to the international neighborhood.

Doo wop singers were faceless.

The anonymity partly accounts for how sadly disposable these acts seemed to be, but it also contributed an innocent, unaffected quality that was inherent to their music. They were just regular people, which seemed to resonate with regular listeners.

Of course, anonymity may not have been exactly what doo wop artists had in mind. There's little doubt that many in their ranks wanted to be pop stars. But the silver lining in that cloud is that music—just music—was the message. Very rarely in the entire past century has music remained untangled from the image of its makers. It's refreshing. It keeps your ears open.

Meanwhile, rock 'n' roll was sending up pop heroes like Hollywood sends up movie stars (and sometimes the rockers were movie stars, too): Elvis Presley, Jerry Lee Lewis, Connie Francis, Buddy Holly, Fats Domino, the Big Bopper, Bobby Rydell, Ritchie Valens…The same machine that produced Bing Crosby to soothe our nerves during the war and Dinah Shore to help us fall asleep on the couch made poster boys of the first rock 'n' roll stars. The era of the individual artist had never ended; it just moved its spotlight.

That was the music industry at work, and sometimes the manufacturing of an image masked the intent or even the talent of an artist. After all, these pop stars didn't pop up out of nowhere— they had music histories of their own. Elvis, a good Southern boy, had been reared on gospel, rhythm & blues and country. Though often criticized for "stealing rock 'n' roll from the black man" (a strange charge, especially since Bill Haley had beaten him to the rock 'n' roll punch anyway), Elvis was in awe of

Doo wop singers were faceless.

The anonymity partly accounts for how sadly disposable these acts seemed to be, but it also contributed an innocent, unaffected quality that was inherent to their music. They were just regular people, which seemed to resonate with regular listeners.

Of course, anonymity may not have been exactly what doo wop artists had in mind. There's little doubt that many in their ranks wanted to be pop stars. But the silver lining in that cloud is that music—just music—was the message. Very rarely in the entire past century has music remained untangled from the image of its makers. It's refreshing. It keeps your ears open.

Meanwhile, rock 'n' roll was sending up pop heroes like Hollywood sends up movie stars (and sometimes the rockers were movie stars, too): Elvis Presley, Jerry Lee Lewis, Connie Francis, Buddy Holly, Fats Domino, the Big Bopper, Bobby Rydell, Ritchie Valens…The same machine that produced Bing Crosby to soothe our nerves during the war and Dinah Shore to help us fall asleep on the couch made poster boys of the first rock 'n' roll stars. The era of the individual artist had never ended; it just moved its spotlight.

That was the music industry at work, and sometimes the manufacturing of an image masked the intent or even the talent of an artist. After all, these pop stars didn't pop up out of nowhere—they had music histories of their own. Elvis, a good Southern boy, had been reared on gospel, rhythm & blues and country. Though often criticized for "stealing rock 'n' roll from the black man" (a strange charge, especially since Bill Haley had beaten him to the rock 'n' roll punch anyway), Elvis was in awe of

Barbie Debuts

With an eye-popping figure bearing no connection to anatomy, Mattel's Barbie doll debuted in 1959 as an alternative to the baby-style dolls of the era. In her tiger-striped swimsuit, she sent the message "Buy me!" and was quickly scooped up by girls nationwide. Massive branding followed and soon she was sharing her perfect life with a handsome boyfriend Ken, enjoying their perky friends Midge and Allan, and creating an entire industry of fashion and accessories. Girls may have secretly wanted to look like Barbie and guys like Ken, but we had plenty of "real life" to deal with. By the way, anyone lucky enough to have held onto their original Barbie doll would in later years be sitting pretty at an online auction site!

The Elegants

A classy quintet from Staten Island, New York, the Elegants supposedly got their name from looking at a whiskey bottle with the word Elegance on it. They had one major hit in 1958, "Little Star."

THE DUBS

The Dubs recorded two doo wop classics, "Don't Ask Me to Be Lonely" and "Could This Be Magic," both written by lead singer Richard Blandon. According to rock 'n' roll mythology, they got their name from the music lingo term meaning a copy of a recording.

The Hollywood Flames

A group with an identity crisis. In a career that lasted a decade and a half, these West Coasters recorded under at least seven names—including the Flames, the Jets, the Satellites and the Tangiers—and for nineteen different record labels.

The Fireflies

A one-hit wonder from Philadelphia, the Fireflies' "You Are Mine" is every teenager's dream of desire. It is a sweet song but not aggressive, and was accepted by parents at the time.

THE RACE FOR SPACE

The intense rivalry between the United States and the Soviet Union to "go where no one has gone before"—better known as the "Space Race"—hit American popular culture like a meteor shower. Outer-space toys flooded the market, NASA-endorsed edibles like Tang and Space Food Sticks were consumed with abandon, while space-themed TV shows and movies (with evil aliens as metaphorical stand-ins for the "Red Menace") were all over the big and small screens. Rocket-styled diners and motel signs lined the interstates, and every kid in the country wanted to be an astronaut when they grew up

It all began in October 1957, with the launch of the Sputnik satellite by the U.S.S.R.

Taking place at the height of the Cold War, Sputnik was a stunning blow to U.S. and NATO technology. Even though the U.S. launched its own satellite, Explorer 1, four months afterwards, and established the National Aeronautics and Space Administration (NASA) in 1958, the Russians maintained their lead. In 1961, they put the first human, Yuri Gagarin, in space. Finally picking up momentum, shortly afterward the U.S. launched its first manned craft, Freedom 7, piloted by astronaut Alan Shepard, , and saw John Glenn successfully orbit the earth in 1962.

While more manned and satellite operations took place in the years to come, the objective of landing a man on the moon became the next prize—one the U.S. claimed on July 21, 1969, when Neil Armstrong became the first human to set foot on the lunar surface.

Rock 'n' roll kept up with the race for space, as evidenced by classics like "Rocket Ship" by Vernon Green and the Medallions, "Rocket" by Joe Bennet and the Sparkletones, and the Tornados' instrumental satellite homage, "Telstar." In Philadelphia and New York, deejay Douglas "Jocko" Henderson, also known as "The Ace from Outer Space," blasted through the airwaves with his popular "Rocket Ship Show."

his musical forefathers. And where did the King turn for back-up vocals? To a quartet of country singers with deep roots in gospel. As history tells it, the Jordanaires were appearing on a regional TV show in Memphis circa 1953, and eighteen-year-old Elvis was enamored with their singing. He somehow managed to get backstage, where he approached the group and said he wanted the group to back him when he hit the big time. The Jordanaires didn't laugh—they took the young man seriously. Elvis kept his word, and from 1956 all the way through 1970 the Jordanaires added soul, country and doo wop stylings to many of Elvis' recordings.

The story is one of many examples of how doo wop helped fertilize rock 'n' roll, and vice versa. Rock had just as righteous a claim to groups like the Del-Vikings, Dion and the Belmonts, Little Anthony and the Imperials, and the Coasters as doo wop did.

Keep it light

Music is the newspaper of our times, and the headlines in the late 1950s carried some good news. In a way, American culture was in its teenage years. The Cold War, McCarthyism and the prior generation's memories of World War II had already scratched the luster off of our innocence, but we were not yet as disillusioned and skeptical as we would learn to become. This was the age of Jack Benny, the Volkswagen Beetle, poodle haircuts and *South Pacific*. Yes, there was a big, bad world out there, but we could take the time to have some fun and cut a rug. In doo wop as in rock 'n' roll, we enjoyed a mix of celebration and escapism.

Lyrics never got much darker than tales of the lovelorn like the narrator in 'Silhouettes' by the Rays.

The Del-Vikings

For all the talent packed into the Del-Vikings, and all the convoluted history, it's amazing that only two hit songs floated to the surface during their tenure. "Come Go with Me" and "Whispering Bells" are strong evidence not only of their musical skills, but of how well-suited they were to maintaining doo wop sensibilities in a world increasingly smitten with rock 'n' roll.

Oddly enough, there was more than just one group using the Del-Vikings name—or some alternate spelling of it—in 1957, when both singles were at the height of airplay and exposure. That's because their manager utilized a loophole in their contract with the small Fee-Bee label to sell them to Mercury Records once "Come Go With Me" went through the roof. The move split the group into rival factions with nearly identical names, though the Mercury version of the Del-Vikings featured the group's founder and bass singer, Clarence E. Quick, who had penned both hits. Things were further confused when a cappella demos the original group had made were re-released with newly

dubbed backing tracks, and it got even one step weirder when another incarnation of the group showed up in the movie *The Big Beat* with Fats Domino. You can imagine how many people were laying claim to royalty checks when their songs were at the top of the charts.

The Del-Vikings had begun as a singing group in the U. S. Air Force, and military commitments had kept their personnel constantly shifting in the early days. But the rivalry and competition was spawned by managers and labels who sought to squeeze all the green they could out of the band once it was clear they were hit-makers. Sadly, the Del-Vikings were like the goose that laid the golden egg: Just those two golden hits made the charts before business interests threatened to kill the goose. The group members eventually settled and reunited, but by that time audiences had moved on. It's still tough to untangle just who is on those old records under the names The Del-Vikings, The Del Vikings, and The Dell-Vikings. When you flip through the CD bins for one of their collections, heads up!

Doo wop was easy to listen to, easy to follow, and easy to sing along to— all key factors in the success of any popular sound.

Nineteen-fifty-eight saw the peak of doo wop airplay, with songs like "Twilight Time" (the Platters), "Lollipop" (the Chordettes), "Get a Job" (the Silhouettes) and "Tears on My Pillow" (Little Anthony and the Imperials) on everyone's lips. Favorites of '59 followed such as "A Teenager in Love" (Dion and the Belmonts), "There Goes My Baby" (the Drifters) and "Smoke Gets in Your Eyes" (the Platters, again). In keeping with rock 'n' roll's mood, the songs were all light fare—nothing too heady or thought-provoking. Doo wop lyrics never got much darker than tales of the lovelorn, like the narrator in "Silhouettes" by the Rays who sees his girl kissing another man through the windowshade (a song that so inspired four gospel singers from Philadelphia that they named their group the Silhouettes).

The nearest relation to a political song may have been when the Drifters were offered a tune called "Only in America," which contained the opening lyric *Only in America / Can a guy from nowhere / Go to sleep a pauper and wake up a millionaire.* But the Drifters refused to sing a song that was a lie to the black experience and turned the tune down, handing a huge hit over to Jay and the Americans. Doo wop did honor its home country in a handful of patriotic soldier songs ("The White Cliffs of Dover" recorded by Lee Andrews and the Hearts, "Pray for Me" by the Four Pharoahs) but the artists were not about to dishonor their heritage.

The Drifters made a statement by not recording the song, but another curiosity of doo wop is how apolitical the genre was. There were no protest songs and no lyrics about social issues or inequality.

FRANK SINATRA AND EDDIE HODGES IN A HOLE IN THE HEAD

The Hula Hoop

Though playing with hoops goes back thousands of years, the plastic hula hoop released by Wham-O in 1958 took the country by storm. Twenty-four million were sold in just the first six months with everyone—young, old, rich, poor—busy twisting and turning while trying to keep the hoop swinging around their bodies. One of the easiest and simplest forms of entertainment ever produced, it made people laugh then, and still does today.

THE ISLEY BROTHERS

In a career that spans decades, the Isley Brothers came from Cincinnati, Ohio, but found fame and fortune on the streets of New York. In 1959 they recorded "Shout, Parts I and II" and rock 'n' roll history was made. "Twist 'n' Shout," "This Old Heart of Mine," "That Lady" and many more followed.

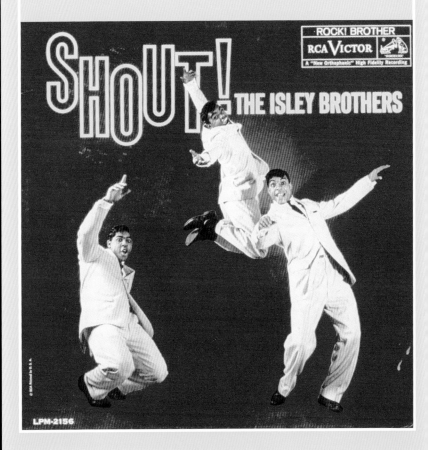

1959: The Day the Music Died

For later generations, "the day the music died" wouldn't mean much more than a phrase from an old Don McLean song. But if you grew up in the 1950s, the story behind the song "American Pie" touched you deep inside.

It was February 1959, and a tour bus full of talent was rolling across the frozen Midwest. The tour, called the Winter Dance Party, featured Buddy Holly & His Crickets, Dion and the Belmonts, Ritchie Valens and J.P. "the Big Bopper" Richardson. The three-week tour was a teenager's dream show and, on February 2nd, made an impromptu stop in Clear Lake, Iowa, to play at the Surf Ballroom.

Dion DiMucci of Dion and the Belmonts has shared his memories with me.

The bus had been cold. Really cold. To keep blood flowing and spirits high, the gang of them would sometimes sing a warm-hearted little song with the lyric *I'm gonna hug my radiator / when I hit my hotel room*. But there wasn't a song worth singing that would get Buddy Holly back on the busted-up bus for that night's six-hour ride to Moorhead, Minnesota. Buddy chartered a single-engine plane to the next tour stop after the Surf Ballroom show.

There were three passenger seats on the small Beechcraft Bonanza airplane. Two of the musicians in the Crickets—bassist Waylon Jennings and guitarist Tommy Allsop—flipped a coin for one of the empty seats. But they knew headliner Ritchie Valens had been having a particularly tough time on the bus. Valens, with Mexican blood and California roots, had not taken well to the Midwest's brutal chill. His parents had in fact sent him a pea coat to stay warm, but he was quite sick. Jennings and Allsop gave Valens the seat.

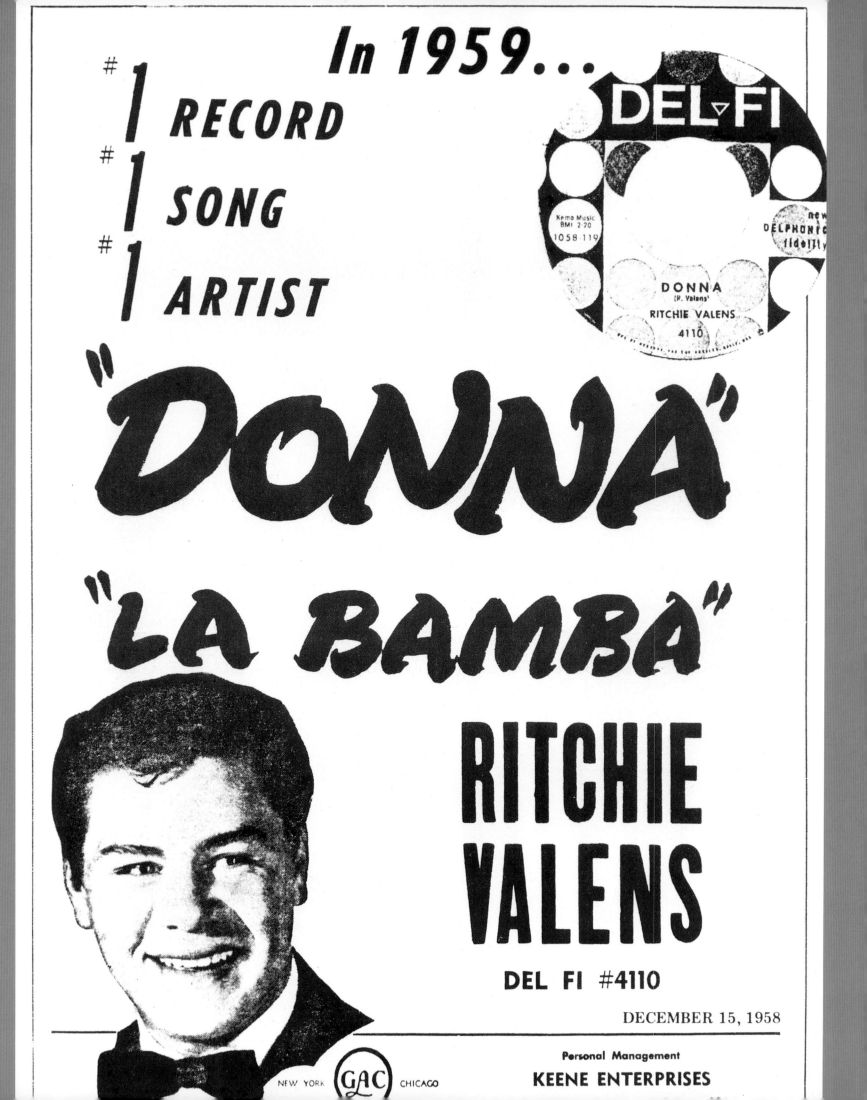

The plane took off at 1:00 AM with pilot Roger Peterson flying passengers Buddy Holly, Ritchie Valens and the Big Bopper. A few minutes later, just five miles northwest of the airport, the Beechcraft went down in a snowy field.

Buddy Holly asked Dion to join him on the plane, at a cost of $36 per seat. Dion remembered how his parents used to argue and worry about paying $36 per month to cover the rent on their Bronx apartment. Hearing his parents in his head, Dion just couldn't bring himself to spend the same money on a quick plane ride. He declined Buddy's invitation, said goodbye, and headed back towards the bus.

The plane took off at 1:00 AM with pilot Roger Peterson flying passengers Buddy Holly, Ritchie Valens, and the Big Bopper. A few minutes later, just five miles northwest of the airport, the Beechcraft went down in a snowy field.

The sadness that came over all the surviving members of the tour was matched only by their guilt. Their fellow musicians, their touring buddies, kindred spirits—lost. Incredibly, the tour went on. Desperately seeking local talent in Moorhead to fill the bill that night, the tour promoters hired a local fifteen-year-old named Bobby Velline since he knew the lyrics to six of Holly's tunes. He took the stage with his brother and a band they called the Shadows, and the audience loved them—as did the executives present from Liberty Records. Bobby Vee's career was launched that night. Vee has always said it was a bittersweet start, and he still plays the Winter Dance Party memorial shows in Clear Lake.

Dion was in shock for weeks and carried the pain in his heart for years. Although he had great success both with and without the Belmonts, he would later go down some dark and very difficult paths. But with the help of friends, family and newfound faith, he eventually found his way back. In the year 2000, with the release of his *Déjà Nu* record, Dion finally had closure with that cold Midwest night.

The album includes two very special tracks. "Everyday (That I'm with You)" is a warm memory of his friendship with Buddy Holly. A tribute to both the man and his music, Dion hits the chorus lyric just like Buddy does on his own classic "Everyday." And, more than forty years after he bounced around the Midwest in that miserable bus with his music-making buddies, Dion committed "Hug My Radiator" to the ages.

Doo wop helped fertilize rock 'n' roll, and vice versa.

Here in the late 1950s, with the civil rights movement gaining steam, no song sang the story. Chart-topping African American artists would sell out venues in towns that refused to rent them a hotel room, yet the musical style contained few messages specific to the politics of the black experience. Look backwards in time and there are songs of adversity, oppression and fear in blues, gospel, R&B and jazz (Billie Holiday's "Strange Fruit" being the supreme example); look forward and you can find the same in Motown, funk, rock and hip-hop. But in doo wop music, even with the spotlight trained on dozens of hit artists, the message skipped a beat. Certainly the music's DNA was woven through with the hardship of the blues, the pleading of gospel and the streetwise edge of R&B. But in doo wop, these were all passive genes.

Shape of things to come

At the doorstep to the 1960s, the rock 'n' roll party was in full swing. Far from the stage lights and dance floors, though, an undercurrent of change was quietly beginning to swell in the cafés and coffee shops. A new generation of poets and performers were beginning to challenge "the establishment" artistically, socially and politically. The newly empowered youth movement was turning into a full-blown youth revolt that would characterize the decade to come.

Looking back, we can spot telltale signs indicating the shape of things to come. Jack Kerouac's *On the Road* had been published in 1957. In 1958, Elvis left for the army. On February 3, 1959, "the day the music died," we lost three cherished stars of rock 'n' roll. For many, the tragedy symbolized the end of an era. Whatever innocence rock 'n' roll had left—or that America had left—was about to end.

The Silhouettes

Recorded by The Silhouettes on EMBER Records
GET A JOB
Words and Music by THE SILHOUETTES

WILDCAT MUSIC and ULYSSES & BAGBY MUSIC
1619 Broadway New York 19, N.Y.

Fame was as unexpected as it was unlikely for the Silhouettes, who had been a church-minded gospel group called the Gospel Tornadoes based in Philadelphia. Since their smash hit was "Get a Job," it seems all too fitting that they wrote and recorded secular songs only to make ends meet. They took their new name from a song by another secular group, the Rays, who sang in "Silhouettes" about a jilted lover who spies his girlfriend in the arms of another man.

"Get a Job" sold over one million copies after its release late in 1957. It topped the pop charts and the R&B charts, and earned the Silhouettes a spot sharing bills with the likes of Jackie Wilson, Paul Anka and Sam Cooke. But success is fleeting in the music biz, and their star fell nearly as quickly as it rose. You can almost follow the group's trajectory in their song titles: "Headin' for the Poorhouse" came out in 1958, and "I Sold My Heart to the Junkman" followed right on its heels! Still, the impossibly low bass hook in "Get a Job" earned the Silhouettes a permanent place in doo wop history.

Little Anthony and the Imperials

The story of how Little Anthony and the Imperials got their name has been passed down through the years, and Anthony Gourdine even likes to tell it himself. One evening in 1958, he was sitting on a park bench near his home in Brooklyn, New York. He was listening Alan Freed, the immortal father of rock 'n' roll radio, spin records on New York's WINS radio. Now, the group had previously recorded as the Duponts and as the Chesters, but at this time they were on End Records as the Imperials. As Freed set up the next record, he announced, "…and here's a new record that's making a lot of noise…Little Anthony and the Imperials singing 'Tears On My Pillow.'"

The on-air name change came as a surprise to Anthony himself—he wasn't even that small! But Freed had broken the record on his show, and the record company's owner liked the catchy name so much that he rush-released the next set of records with new labels. From that day forward, the name stuck.

"Tears" reached the Top 10. The record's B-side was another ballad called "Two Kinds Of People," and it, too, became a hit. The rare one-two punch marked the beginning of a long and terrific career. The group had extraordinary success even after doo wop's heyday passed, garnering hits such as "I'm On The Outside (Looking In)," "Goin' Out Of My Head" and "Hurt So Bad" well into the 1960s.

There's another story about the group that I like to tell. The song "Shimmy Shimmy Ko-Ko Bop" was a huge hit for them in 1959 and 1960. It was kind of a novelty song—a fun, faddy thing released at a time when pop music was all about dancing. I was on air at WABC radio, and we sent out a dance sheet of how to do the Shimmy Shimmy Ko-Ko Bop dance. I sent out 25,000 initial copies—and within a week, there were so many requests that we had to double-print the sheet. Over fifty thousand people wanted it. Years later I was asked to write the liner notes for an Imperials collection, and one of the songs on it was "Shimmy Shimmy Ko-Ko Bop." Anthony came to me and said, "Do you have to include that in the collection? I hate that song!" Because Anthony and the guys were serious performers, the song probably seemed a little silly to them. But I did like it, and I play it to this day. And I still know how to do the Ko-Ko Bop dance.

To call these guys a great group is short-changing them. Far beyond the fun stories and a quirky dance hit, their harmonies, stage presence and choreography were all fantastic. They survived the 1950s, had a thriving career in the '60s and have even survived in this new millennium. Their staying power is unsurpassed because their music is just timeless. Little Anthony and the Imperials didn't depend on anything that had come before—everything they did had the future in it.

Battle of the Groups

end
HIGH FIDELITY

LP 305

THE FLAMINGOS

THE IMPERIALS

THE DUBS

ISLEY BROS.

LITTLE ANTHONY
AND **THE IMPERIALS**

SHIMMY SHIMMY KO-KO BOP

Words and Music by BOB SMITH

RECORDED ON END RECORDS BY LITTLE ANTHONY AND THE IMPERIALS

RECORD MUSIC, INC.

Sole Selling Agent:

CRITERION MUSIC CORP.

1270 6th Ave.,   Radio City, N. Y.

Brigitte Bardot

Mon dieu! It was 1957 when America laid eyes on Brigitte Bardot in the film *And God Created Woman*, and men across the country immediately stood at attention. The U.S. had enjoyed its fair share of beauty queens over the years, but this French seductress was in many ways our first sex symbol. If the phrase "sex kitten" had ever been uttered before, it was never so fitting. She was feline and exotic, she hissed at conventional mores and she purred in a luscious accent that drove men nuts.

And God Created Woman, which was directed by Roger Vadim (whom Bardot married when she was eighteen), carried the tag line "…but the devil created Brigitte Bardot." The idea of Bardot as Satan's plaything guaranteed both her stardom and her condemnation. As much as we like to think of social life in the U.S. as liberal and free, we've always been pretty high strung in terms of sex. It was a scandal when Europe exported its sexuality by way of sensuous, strong women like France's Bardot and Italy's Sophia Loren. Bardot, who had been modeling since the age of fifteen and had already made a dozen movies in France, was too provocative even for Hollywood. Being society's favorite taboo was a great burden on her; so much so that in September of 1960 she attempted suicide—on her twenty-sixth birthday—by swallowing pills and slitting her wrists. Years later, on her fiftieth birthday, Bardot would tell *The London Times*, "I have been very happy, very rich, very beautiful, much adulated, very famous and very unhappy."

As usual, the story behind the headlines is not as pretty as the front-page picture. But Brigitte Bardot helped loosen a nation that was just learning not to be so uptight.

Known to turn a man into an animal, Brigitte Bardot is famously quoted: "Men are beasts and even beasts don't behave as they do."

the teddy bears

Phil Spector is famous for creating the "Wall of Sound," but before that he was a struggling musician and a Teddy Bear. That all changed when the Los Angeles-based trio recorded one of his compositions "To Know Him is to Love Him" in 1958, which was supposedly a dedication to his late father.

THE MONOTONES

This sextet from Newark, New Jersey, was a classic one-hit wonder, but what a hit it was. According to legend, the distinctive bass-drum slam on the intro to "Book Of Love" (*Oh I wonder wonder/oom ba-doo-oo who—WHUMP!*) may have been inspired by a baseball crashing through the recording-studio window right on cue.

HANK BALLARD
AND
THE MIDNIGHTERS

A member of the Rock and Roll Hall of Fame, Hank Ballard was a major force in shaping the course of rock. He started the "Annie" song craze with "Work with Me Annie" and also wrote and recorded "The Twist," probably the most influential dance record ever. However, it was Ernest Evans, aka Chubby Checker, who shot to glory as his version reached #1 and got everyone under 180 twisting and turning.

THE BLUE NOTES

DANNY AND THE JUNIORS

A great example of the early Philadelphia R&B sound, the Blue Notes had a regional hit called "If You Love Me" but scored later with "My Hero." By the time Teddy Pendergrass joined up in 1970, they were known as Harold Melvin and the Blue Notes, turning out hits like "If You Don't Know Me By Now."

Originally titled "Do the Bop" after a current dance craze, Danny and the Junior's "At the Hop" was a sensation. Both "Hop" and their follow-up record "Rock and Roll is Here to Stay" are rock 'n' roll standards, but the sentimental ballad "Sometimes When I Am Alone" is as enticing as any doo wop song of the time.

THE OLYMPICS

The Olympics came out of Los Angeles and expertly mixed doo wop with rock 'n' roll. Perhaps true to their Hollywood roots, they released "Western Movies" as a spoof of the genre and wrangled an international hit.

THE FIESTAS

Neighborhood friends who grew up together in Newark, New Jersey, the Fiestas were signed to Old Town records by president Hy Weiss. Their biggest hit was 1959's "So Fine."

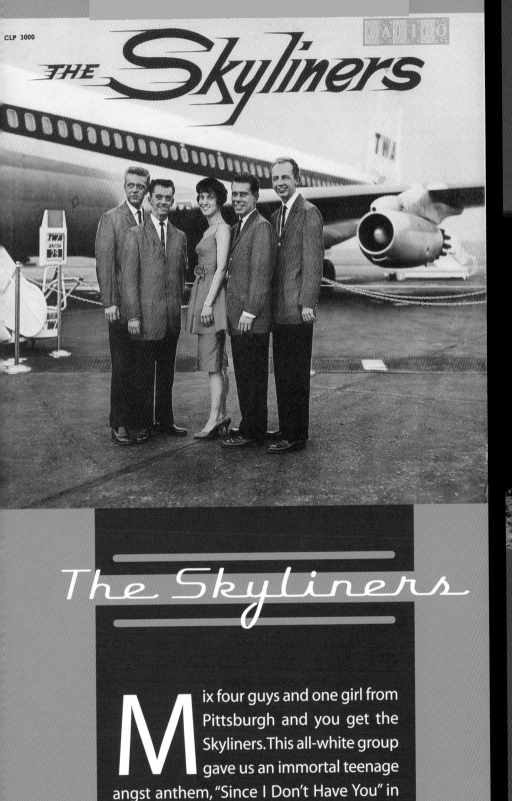

The Skyliners

Mix four guys and one girl from Pittsburgh and you get the Skyliners. This all-white group gave us an immortal teenage angst anthem, "Since I Don't Have You" in 1958. Their 1960 version of "Pennies From Heaven" also spent some time on the charts.

THE ROYAL TEENS

First called the Royal Tones, the group changed their name to the Royal Teens because—no surprise here—they were all teenagers. They had one huge hit in 1958, the quirky "Short Shorts," and shortly after that went bye-bye.

The Chantels

Why were there so few all-girl groups? One of the reasons is that it wasn't very nice, in those days, for "girls" to be on the road. It was a rough lifestyle, full of rough characters. Even the young women who could take it would have a tough time convincing their families to let them go out on tour in a bus full of guys.

But Arlene Smith and the Chantels got out there all right, and they're still out there today. They had a deeply romantic sound, though their biggest hits are melancholy declarations of unrequited love: "He's Gone" and "Maybe" provided the soundtrack as countless broken-hearted teenage girls cried into their pillows.

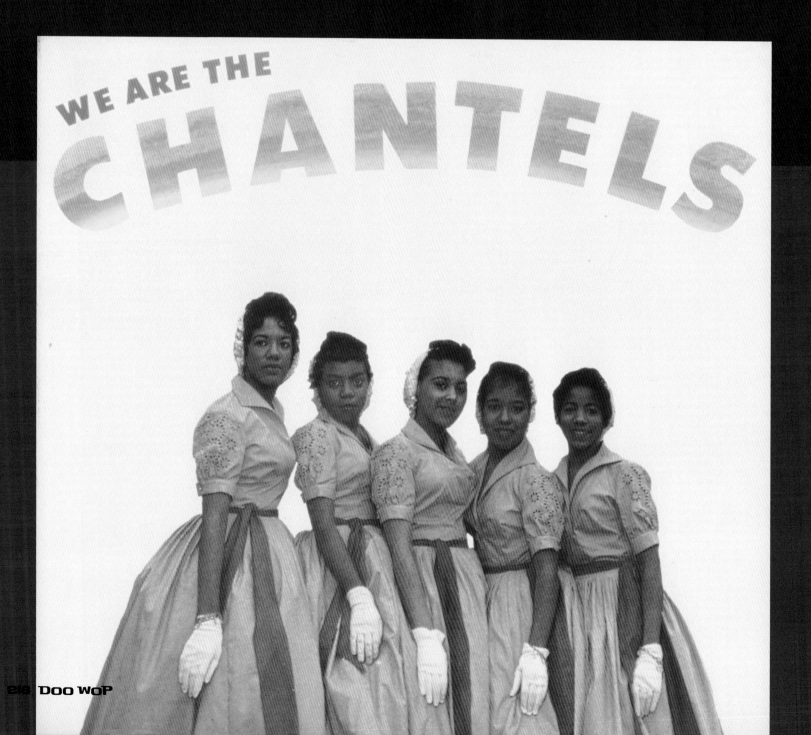

The "Jive Bombers"

"EARL" "PEEWEE" "AL" "CLARENCE"

The Jive Bombers

THE QUIN-TONES

A rare mix of four girls and one guy, the Philadelphia-based Quin-Tones' claim to fame was their wedding anthem "Down the Aisle of Love" which opened with an organ version of "Here Comes the Bride."

Before forming the Jive Bombers in 1952, lead singer Clarence Palmer sang with big band acts in the 1940s. Infusing R&B with jazz gave the Bombers a distinctive sound. Their 1957 hit "Bad Boy" was written by Avon Long and Lillian Armstrong, a former wife of Louis Armstrong.

QUINTONES

The Quiz Show Scandal

$64,000

GE ELECTRIC

WINNER JOYCE MYRON

Television had just recently become a fixture of American life when the quiz show scandal broke in 1958. Shows like *The $64,000 Question* and *Dotto* came under fire when it was revealed they had been rigged for high drama, but it was Jack Barry's *Twenty-One* that history remembers most notoriously. Two years after his 1956 loss to professor Charles Van Doren, contestant Herb Stempel—who had been coached by producers himself—blew the whistle on the show.

We had all been drawn into the contest between the two, rooting for Van Doren the underdog to beat out Stempel the brainiac. We wanted to believe in Van Doren. But the questions, the responses, the dramatic staging—all of it was manufactured. Even our response to Van Doren had been manipulated; the producers had banked on national favor resting with the handsome Van Doren and had Stempel take a dive.

No one ever dreamed that someone behind the curtain was fudging the rules or feeding answers to a contestant. After all, we had been brought up on trust and had invited this entertainment into our own living rooms, like we had with Uncle Miltie. It was a time in which we trusted our government, trusted our local politicians, trusted the clergy and trusted each other.

The quiz show scandal was an awakening for Americans. It sounds weird that a hokey quiz show on television would mean so much, but it weakened us. It's the very first time we were let down on a national level like this. Everyone was so excited and involved, and then we found out that it was all rigged. It's wasn't the American way. The scandal was a sad moment in our history—an early chink in the armor, and a warning of things to come.

Maurice Williams and The Gladiolas

It's just about impossible to hear the bouncy and breathless "Little Darlin'" without a big smile coming over your face. Maurice Williams penned the hit for his Gladiolas, and it was one of the first times that a Latin-inflected rhythm crossed over into rock 'n' roll's mainstream. The Diamonds, a white doo wop act from Ontario known for covers, took the song all the way to #2 in 1957 (with Elvis blocking at #1 with "All Shook Up") while the Gladiolas only reached #41. Though Williams was bested with his own song, the Diamonds have since proven to be gracious winners, giving credit to Williams for their greatest success and inviting him to share their spotlight onstage.

Williams and the Gladiolas were from South Carolina, which is unusual since you can probably count on one hand the number of doo wop groups from south of the Mason-Dixon Line. Success and recognition were hard won for the Gladiolas; not only did the Diamonds run away with their hit, but a legal issue robbed them of their name. They changed to Maurice Williams and the Zodiacs in 1959, and finally hoisted themselves on their own petard with "Stay" in 1960. The song was an instant smash and has been revisited many times. The Zodiacs' own version was revived on the 1987 soundtrack to *Dirty Dancing* and has been lovingly covered by the Hollies, the Beach Boys, the Four Seasons, Rufus and Chaka Khan, and perhaps most famously by Jackson Browne.

16 CANDLES' THE CRESTS

When you listen to the Crests you are sampling some of the very best that doo wop has to offer, and you also get a glimpse of where our music was headed at the time. "My Juanita," "Sixteen Candles"—these records had everything a rock 'n' roll record should have to appeal to teenagers, plus enough energy and emotion to carry older audiences as well.

This was the band that reared Johnny Maestro, one of the finest, most spirited, most emotional voices in all of rock 'n' roll. Johnny now sings with the Brooklyn Bridge, and he is always true to the emotion of the recordings made back in the late '50s. He's just a natural, with a wonderful ability to weave through the harmonies. He can make you laugh and make you smile; he can make you dance in "Step By Step" or bring a tear to your eye with "The Worst That Could Happen." The Crests had a terrific little band behind them, too, and they all blended so well with the percussion, strings, guitars and horns they experimented with. They just had the perfect formula.

The Crests also deserve mention for being remarkably integrated, which was rare back in the '50s. The group featured two African American guys, one African American girl, one Puerto Rican, and one Italian. Any guesses where Maestro fit in that melting pot? Well, this ought to give it away: Johnny Maestro was born John Mastrangelo.

ELVIS PRESLEY IN KING CREOLE

hello elvis

In addition to being the King of Rock 'n' Roll—not to mention just about the biggest name in twentieth century popular music—Elvis Presley was everyone's American Dream come true. He came from a very poor family but had a vision he worked on for years, one that he actually achieved. And during that time he gave our society so much pleasure.

Never before had there been an entertainer with Elvis's charisma or magical ability to draw people in. Elvis was good looking and had all the right moves—moves that gave everyone who saw him perform a real sense of freedom. He really put his whole body into it; "Elvis the Pelvis," people called him. It all seems so tame now, but back then it got a lot of people upset. Especially a lot of parents, who called him vulgar. In fact, their outcry was such that in 1957, for Elvis's final appearance on *The Ed Sullivan Show*, the network ordered its cameramen to shoot him only from the waist up!

Elvis wasn't the first white artist to be heavily influenced by black rhythm and blues, but in his pre-RCA days on Sam Phillips' Sun label in Memphis, Elvis had done something his contemporaries hadn't: fuse

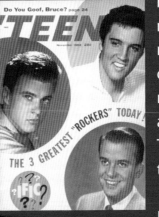

black R&B with white honky-tonk country. In doing this, he created the fiery rockabilly sound, the very template of rock 'n' roll as we know it.

Elvis Presley started the rock 'n' roll business and, with manager Colonel Parker, also made it into big business. Mass-merchandising, movie roles, private jets, Las Vegas residences—these things are now common in the world of rock music. But today's rock stars have a certain gyrating singer from Tupelo, Mississippi, to thank for their lucrative lifestyles.

Yet, no matter how dramatic Elvis's life and career became, he never lost the down-home charm he learned from his humble parents, Vernon and Gladys Presley. He was the perfect gentleman to me and I loved playing his music. Unfortunately, at the end of his years Elvis was surrounded by people who didn't take care of him, and it was terrible the way his life ended. But during his days here on Earth, he made some of the greatest music of all time—music that will make many people happy for generations to come.

CARY GRANT IN NORTH BY NORTHWEST

hello elvis

In addition to being the King of Rock 'n' Roll—not to mention just about the biggest name in twentieth century popular music—Elvis Presley was everyone's American Dream come true. He came from a very poor family but had a vision he worked on for years, one that he actually achieved. And during that time he gave our society so much pleasure.

Never before had there been an entertainer with Elvis's charisma or magical ability to draw people in. Elvis was good looking and had all the right moves—moves that gave everyone who saw him perform a real sense of freedom. He really put his whole body into it; "Elvis the Pelvis," people called him. It all seems so tame now, but back then it got a lot of people upset. Especially a lot of parents, who called him vulgar. In fact, their outcry was such that in 1957, for Elvis's final appearance on *The Ed Sullivan Show*, the network ordered its cameramen to shoot him only from the waist up!

Elvis wasn't the first white artist to be heavily influenced by black rhythm and blues, but in his pre-RCA days on Sam Phillips' Sun label in Memphis, Elvis had done something his contemporaries hadn't: fuse black R&B with white honky-tonk country. In doing this, he created the fiery rockabilly sound, the very template of rock 'n' roll as we know it.

Elvis Presley started the rock 'n' roll business and, with manager Colonel Parker, also made it into big business. Mass-merchandising, movie roles, private jets, Las Vegas residences—these things are now common in the world of rock music. But today's rock stars have a certain gyrating singer from Tupelo, Mississippi, to thank for their lucrative lifestyles.

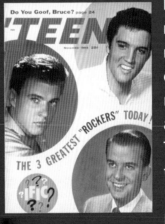

Yet, no matter how dramatic Elvis's life and career became, he never lost the down-home charm he learned from his humble parents, Vernon and Gladys Presley. He was the perfect gentleman to me and I loved playing his music. Unfortunately, at the end of his years Elvis was surrounded by people who didn't take care of him, and it was terrible the way his life ended. But during his days here on Earth, he made some of the greatest music of all time—music that will make many people happy for generations to come.

CHARLTON HESTON AND STEPHEN BOYD IN BEN-HUR

Big-Theme Movies: Epics, Thrillers and Gimmicks

The 1950s were the first decade Hollywood studios had to seriously compete with their rapidly encroaching nemesis, television. Every trick in the book was invoked to pull audiences into the theaters, including the "bigger is best" school of movie making. Lavish Biblical epics like *The Robe*, *Quo Vadis* and *Ben-Hur*, featuring Charlton Heston pounding his way to victory in its classic chariot race, filled every inch of screen with spectacle, all without the aid of today's computer-generated graphics. Alfred Hitchcock's brilliant thriller *North by Northwest* took us on an edge-of-your-seat race from Manhattan to Mount Rushmore with Eva Marie Saint and Cary Grant, who had a near-fatal run-in with a crop dusting plane. Meanwhile, we gladly went *Around the World in Eighty Days* and enjoyed watching Deborah Kerr and Burt Lancaster show us how to make out on the beach in *From Here to Eternity*.

Then there were the gimmicks! Cinerama promised new and thrilling sensations and 3D, though cumbersome, was a lot of fun–particularly with Vincent

DEBORAH KERR AND BURT LANCASTER IN FROM HERE TO ETERNITY

Price doing his monster thing in *House of Wax* and other horror movies. It was shades, or scents, of things to come as evidenced by even more ambitious trickery like Smell-O-Vision. Meanwhile, Marilyn Monroe, Grace Kelly and Ava Gardner brought our temperatures up while tough guys Kirk Douglas, Richard Widmark and William Holden kept us ready for action.

It was also a decade of slowly shaking off the draconian Production Code that had censored all but the most "proper" onscreen morals and ethics. In John Ford's classic western *The Searchers*, John Wayne plays a man driven by racism and revenge while *The Man with the Golden Arm* deals with drug addiction. Racial prejudice is also a major theme of *The Defiant Ones*, starring Sidney Poitier and Tony Curtis. The rise of Method acting brought us Marlon Brando, Montgomery Clift and the doomed James Dean, who helped usher in the first youth-oriented movies—a genre that, for better or worse, is thriving today. Yes, it was quite a decade.

Gimmicks were everywhere.
Cinerama promised
thrilling sensations and 3D,
though cumbersome,
was a lot of fun.

The Velours

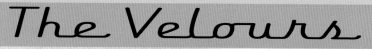

THE VELOURS

A tight Brooklyn street corner group, the Velours had one hit in 1957, "Can I Come Over Tonight." Though it was enough to get them on the tour circuit, they never surpassed the popularity of that release.

TONIGHT-TONIGHT
the Mellokings

THE MELLOKINGS

An all-white group with a near-black sound, the Mellokings scored in 1957 with "Tonight Tonight," a classic ballad that is considered one of favorite songs of the decade, and just right for romance.

THE CELLOS

Singing on the street corners of New York honed their R&B skills, but the Cellos had only one hit: "Rang Tang Ding Dong." A novelty song that cracked the Billboard Top 100, "Rang Tang Ding Dong" inspired them to try other novelty records, but without much success.

THE IMPALAS

An interracial group from Brooklyn, New York, The Impalas' ticket to touring and television appearances with big-time acts was their one hit "Sorry, I Ran All the Way Home."

The Mystics

A talented Brooklyn street corner group, the Mystics are fondly remembered for their huge hit "Hushabye" and appeared many times with me at Palisades Amusement Park. A beautiful song with near-perfect harmonies, "Hushabye" has been covered over the years by many artists, but none has matched the original.

the Pastels

Formed while serving in the U.S. Air Force in Greenland of all places, the Pastels kept warm by practicing their sizzling vocal harmonies. Once back in the U.S. in 1957, they released "Been So Long," "You Don't Love Me Anymore" and "So Far Away."

THE RAYS

THE RAYS

A Brooklyn-based group that is best remembered for the classic "Silhouettes." Formed with ex-members of the Four Fellows, the Rays were in the right place at the right time when producer/writer Bob Crewe decided they were the group to record what has become one of the best known songs in rock history.

The Bobettes

One of rock's first girl groups to hit it big, the Bobbettes were a quintet of teenagers from Harlem. Originally called the Harlem Queens, they sang at local parties and functions and appeared at the legendary Apollo Theater's Amateur Night. Manager James Dailey changed their name and directed them to a monster debut hit with "Mr. Lee," named for one of their school teachers.

CHAPTER 6
1960 – 1963

Redirection

N o one saw it coming. Maybe older generations expected America's teenagers to grow out of their crazy rock 'n' roll fad just like they'd grow out of their hairdos and their bobby socks and their weirdo dances. The kids couldn't really mean it when they sang "Rock 'n' Roll is Here to Stay" along with Danny and the Juniors… could they?

Parents plugged their ears and waited for it all to end, but rock 'n' roll was gaining a head of steam. In the early '60s it was becoming clear that the music wasn't part of a craze, it was part of a culture, and the coming-of-age Baby Boomers provided that culture with a massive population base. The teenage experience was playing out on a national scale: In the same way an eighteen-year-old defies the rules laid down

The teenage experience was playing out on a national scale.

by Mother and Father, an entire generation was questioning the authority and judgment of its leaders. The very identity of America was being challenged, and over the course of the 1960s it would be completely re-thought, redefined and redirected by the young.

Iconography

Like revolutionary leaders in a crowd of rebels, pop icons emerged from the bumper crop of singers, songwriters and groups making music at the turn of the decade. Some are best identified as teen idols and celebrities; guys like Frankie Avalon, Bobby Rydell and Fabian owed their success as much to being handsome as to being talented. Meanwhile, the dyed-in-the-wool musicians were rocking our socks off. After Chubby Checker kick-started the 1960s with

"The Twist," major hits rolled out one after the next from the likes of Ray Charles, Roy Orbison, Duane Eddy, Neil Sedaka, Fats Domino, Del Shannon, Jackie Wilson and Elvis, Elvis, Elvis.

The record industry threw its weight behind rock's royalty. These were natural heroes to the young and, as individual artists, many had a ready-made image that was ideal for marketing, promotion and sales. For the music business, they were the ticket to satisfying audiences on an ever-increasing scale.

None of this was panning out especially well for doo wop artists. For starters, they were accustomed to sharing the limelight among four or five members. Doo wop was founded on multi-part harmonies, so leadmen like Dion DiMucci and Clyde McPhatter were the rare exceptions who could, potentially, be packaged and branded.

Camelot:
The Kennedy White House

John F. Kennedy's tenure as our 35th president was tragically cut short, but the days he occupied the White House were heady ones.

Dubbed "the Camelot years" (a reference to the Broadway musical he had so enjoyed), Kennedy's administration only lasted from 1961 to 1963. Those years, however, were filled with magical fairytale allure, tense international drama and an inspiring spirit of national confidence not seen since.

Burning with charisma, John Fitzgerald Kennedy was America's golden prince. A handsome war hero and at 43, the youngest man to ever take the nation's highest oath, JFK seemed to have it all. He came from a powerful Boston political family, and his beautiful wife, Jacqueline Kennedy, with her striking Chanel suits and pillbox hats, set fashion trends. At times, the life of the Kennedys was more sensational than any soap opera on television.

Once in office, Kennedy quickly proved himself a strong world leader. While the misguided Bay of Pigs invasion of Cuba was a low point, his refusal to back down against Soviet leader Nikita Khrushchev during the Cuban Missile Crisis probably helped avert a nuclear war, and his 1963 Berlin speech promoting democracy stirred millions. He gave the country an amazing image boost at a time when we really needed it.

But despite the serious issues we faced in the early '60s, the Kennedy years were also marked by a rich mood of domestic optimism. His inaugural address, with its famous line, "Ask not what your country can do for you; ask what you can do for your country," moved us all and made us want to do better as a nation. And for one brief, shining moment, as the lyrics of Camelot's theme recall, John F. Kennedy showed us that we could.

The Jive Five

"**M**y True Story" was the 1961 hit by this street-corner group from New York City's borough of Brooklyn. The genuine doo wop sound was becoming scarce early in the 1960s, and the success of the Jive Five is a testimony to their talent and taste, especially for leader Eugene Pitt.

The rest of doo wop's cast was by and large unidentifiable, as far as the industry was concerned. Dion and Clyde McPhatter were two of the few, in fact, who survived by having a go on their own.

Second, doo wop was nice music. Being soft, safe and familiar had helped send the style to the very top in 1958, but now the fans wanted a whole lotta shakin' going on. There was still plenty of room for love songs—there always was and always will be—but the youth market was gaining an appetite for something a little grittier, a little more risqué. If adults had any taste for the mellower side of rock 'n' roll, they did a good job hiding it. And here's where doo wop got into some deep trouble, because the parents who rejected "the devil's music" were gaining an affinity for the innocent strains of doo wop. Your parents like it? Ewwww!

Goldies, not Oldies

Ironically, it was an attempt to promote doo wop that fed the parental problem. I trace it back to the advent of doo wop compilation albums, particularly a batch called Oldies But Goodies released by Art Laboe, the Los Angeles disc jockey and record producer. His compilations sold very well, and thanks to him, singles like "Earth Angel" and "In the Still of the Night" enjoyed an encore at the cash register and on radio. But Laboe's series were marketed as a walk down memory lane or a nostalgic glimpse at days gone by. They put a bookend on doo wop when there were still more volumes to be written.

Plus, words can be potent. Saying "oldies" or "golden oldies" was, in my opinion, very degrading. It hadn't

In the early '60s it was becoming clear that the music wasn't part of a craze, it was part of a culture.

The term 'oldie' turned those songs into museum pieces.

been used in music before; a dated tune by Count Basie or Sinatra would be referred to as classic or timeless. When I hear "oldie," I picture mold and cobwebs. It's disrespectful.

Laboe was a radio man, and his phrase "golden oldie" had its origins in studio lingo. Record racks at each studio contained hundreds of singles standing on end, so jocks and programmers loosely categorized them by putting colored tape on their paper sleeves. Current records went unmarked, but if a single was still in rotation about eight weeks later, a green label identified it as a "recurrent hit." After a year, we'd give it a gold label—hence, "golden oldie."

The term "oldie" turned those songs into museum pieces. Consider how disposably our society treats old people. At a time when the entire nation was becoming centered on youth, identifying doo wop as "old" was like retiring the whole genre.

To make matters worse, doo wop style was even starting to look dated. Rabid fans of rock 'n' roll were always dying to have a glance at their stars, but the relative anonymity of doo wop groups made it tougher for them to get booked on big TV shows like *American Bandstand* and *The Ed Sullivan Show*. (And, really, does anyone remember rock 'n' roll on television before Elvis and the Beatles played Sullivan's show?) There was also a new expectation that groups would be self-contained, since the members of rock 'n' roll bands all played their own instruments. As beautiful as the vocal harmony groups sounded, the image of four men in satiny suits doing the box step was nearly passé.

THE COMPUTER

More than any other technological innovation of the last century, it is the computer that has changed the way we live. Whether we're guiding a Mars Rover, deciphering genetic statistics or just e-mailing the relatives, computers are a regular part of our daily lives. But when commercial computers first came on the scene in the 1950s it was like something from *Captain Video* coming off the TV screen: These great big things with wheels and wires and tubes were going to do our thinking for us?

Although the basic concept of the computer dates back at least to ancient Greece and China, the innovations that led to the first commercial models came about during World War II, when early computing devices were developed for use by the military. But after the war, the Eckert-Mauchly Computer Corporation's UNIVAC 1— known as simply "the UNIVAC"—became the first American computer made exclusively for administrative and business purposes.

The UNIVAC wasn't the only name in the new computer business. Its chief competitor, IBM, used a method of storing information on cheaper and more widely used punch cards instead of UNIVAC's costly metal tape, and would dominate the field by the early 1960s. Today we have computers that quite literally fit in the palms of our hands, but back then the giant UNIVAC was king.

Ed Sullivan Entertains Us

Every Sunday night from 1948 to 1971, millions of Americans of all ages were glued to their television sets for one reason: *The Ed Sullivan Show*. Hosted by the famously stiff ex-vaudeville emcee and newspaper columnist, who nevertheless came across as a quirky but favorite uncle, the show was originally titled *Talk of the Town*. To this day, it remains the longest-running variety program in TV history.

Like clockwork, each week Sullivan presented—as he so wonderfully announced—"a reeeeally big shoe" with an incredibly diverse range of talent—everything from dancing bears to comedians, opera singers, gymnasts and orators.

But between those acts booked to appeal to moms and dads were history-making early appearances by such artists as Elvis Presley, the Beatles and the Rolling Stones. As rock 'n' roll gained in popularity, producers saw gold and the music became a regular attraction on the broadcast. Record labels and talent agencies clamored to get bookings for their acts, since one primetime slot on the nationally airing show could mean more than a dozen appearances on any other program—plus increased record sales.

Who among those sitting in front of the TV on Sunday nights in the '50s or '60s can forget those iconic *Ed Sullivan Show* segments of a gyrating young Elvis singing "Hound Dog," or the screaming girls nearly drowning out the Beatles as the quartet chirped its way through "I Want to Hold Your Hand"? In fact, the night the Beatles made their American TV debut it was reported that there wasn't one teenage crime in the country—all the kids were at home, watching *The Ed Sullivan Show*!

Although his program was eventually overtaken by newer, hipper variety shows like *Laugh-In* and *The Flip Wilson Show*, many U.S. teens got their first taste of rock 'n' roll from Ed Sullivan.

THE BEATLES WITH ED SULLIVAN

SURF'S UP! GIDGET AND THE RISE OF THE SURF CULTURE

Shortly after the publication of *Gidget: The Little Girl with Big Ideas*, Hollywood was ready to ride the wave of the Southern California surf culture and put into production the first of three Gidget movies starring Sandra Dee as Gidget and James Darren as Moondoggie, her surfer-boy love interest. A celebration of endless fun in the sun, Gidget was a sensation with teenagers nationwide, inspiring a slew of similar movies to follow.

"Mouseketeer" Annette Funicello and Frankie Avalon made a series of beach party films including the memorably titled *Beach Blanket Bingo*. It was all a beautiful sun-drenched fantasy. There was all that sand and surf, plus everyone looking great, particularly the gals in their bikinis. These perennial beach partyers had no real worries except how to hold onto your girlfriend or boyfriend, and when to catch the next big wave.

SANDRA DEE (GIDGET) WITH JAMES DARREN (MOONDOOGIE) AND CLIFF ROBERTSON (THE BIG KAHUNA)

BEACH PARTY SCENE FROM OUT OF SIGHT

The Blue Jays

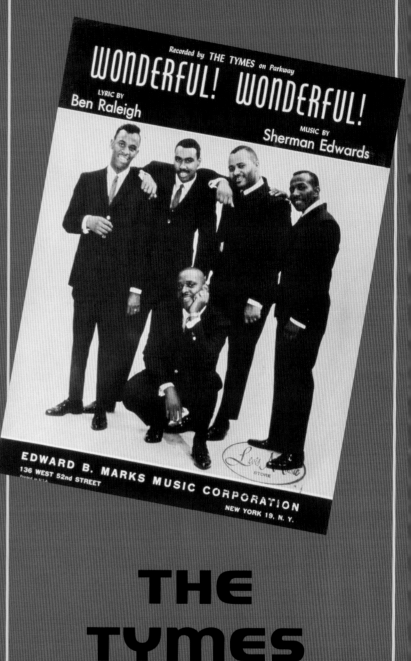

THE TYMES

"Lover's Island" was a tender ballad from 1961. With a romantic lilt cut through by Leon Peels' sharp falsetto, the Blue Jays managed to capture just enough fantasy to set teenagers dreaming of love all that summer.

A prime example of the Philadelphia sound, the Tymes were smooth balladeers. Signed to Parkway Records after a producer caught their act on a Philly talent show, the group hit with "So Much in Love."

Doo wop had enjoyed a ride in rock 'n' roll's sidecar, but it was in danger of being run off the road.

Laid Low by Payola

No discussion on the history of doo wop or rock 'n' roll would be complete without at least a mention of the first payola scandal. The subject does hit a little close to home with me, since disc jockeys were on the hot seat, but this is no personal aside. Payola shook the music industry and the world of radio, and its aftershocks were felt far beyond the station studios and broadcasting towers.

Back in 1958, it had come to the surface that songs were not reaching radio airwaves based on their artistic merit alone: The record industry was paying for exposure. Record promoters, the emissaries of record labels whose job it was to get their label's music played on radio, had taken to bribing disc jockeys. Though the controversial practice had begun much more innocently years before, jocks were now being plied with cash, gifts, trips and more than a few notorious parties.

When payola was uncovered, legislators came down hard. The Federal Trade Commission (a government agency responsible for consumer protection) launched a massive investigation, which in turn led to national headlines damning the reputation of the entire music industry. Heads would roll, for sure, and the first necks on the line were the jocks'. Alan Freed became the poster boy for payola because everyone knew his name, but I think history has been a little too cruel in singling him out. The father of rock 'n' roll pled

The Marcels

With all the bird groups flying around, the Marcels choose to name themselves after a hairstyle worn by one of their members. Their remake of the Rodgers and Hart standard "Blue Moon" earned them a place in doo wop history.

The payola scandal paralyzed radio.

guilty to accepting bribes totaling more than $30,000—but he was only one of many accused. At the height of the investigations in 1960, deejays in major markets like New York, Boston, Chicago and Los Angeles were accused of accepting everything from money and jewelry to drugs and sometimes even "favors" delivered by call girls (I guess those guys were caught in "undercover" operations). Sometimes they were tried by the feds and found guilty; sometimes, just being accused was enough to snuff out a good man's career.

Musical McCarthyism

Thanks to the practice of payola, we learned that repeat plays of a song are nearly an airtight guarantee that a single will sell in droves. It's like a subtle form a brainwashing: This song is haunting me—I must own it! Anyone who has ever had a song stuck in their head whether they like the tune or not knows what I'm talking about. Air time was the motivation behind payola, and repetitive playing (or "heavy rotation") has been used and abused by honorable and less-than-honorable purveyors of music for half a century now.

The fallout from payola might have all been manageable—regrettable, embarrassing and tragic, but manageable—had the threat of legal and public prosecution not paralyzed radio. Fear spread like fire. Everyone became paranoid about fines, jail, and losing their jobs, and stations worried they could lose their licenses to broadcast. As soon as it all hit the fan, upper

THE CHIMES

Once in a while, it just takes a great voice and a good idea to score a hit—and that's how Lenny Cocco took the Chimes to the top with "Once in a While." It was lead-man Lenny's idea to cover the Tommy Dorsey Orchestra's hit from 1937, a wise notion they repeated by covering another old standard, "I'm in the Mood for Love," for another mark on the charts.

Play **TAG** with the Winning Combination

THE CHIMES

I'M IN THE MOOD FOR LOVE

ONLY LOVE

Picked by all the tradepapers as a hit!

TAG 445

Our Sincere Thanks to the nation's DJ's, dealers and operators for making "Once In A While" such a big hit. We hope you'll TAG-a-long with our newest release.

EXCLUSIVELY

TAG RECORDS

A DIVISION OF MUSE PRODUCTS
659 Tenth Ave., New York City

Personal Management
BERGER, ROSS & STEINMAN
15 E. 48th St., N. Y. C.

COMING ATTRACTION:
WATCH FOR OUR FIRST LP

No one old enough today can forget where they were and what they were doing on November 22, 1963, when they heard that President John F. Kennedy had been shot and killed in Dallas, Texas. I was in Brooklyn, driving along Coney Island Avenue near Kings Highway when the news came on the radio. I had to pull over and was so shocked my eyes flooded with tears. It was an hour before I was able to pull myself together enough to continue driving.

Kennedy was visiting Dallas to raise funds for his upcoming re-election campaign and to help quell infighting between Texas Democratic Party members. After arriving by plane, Kennedy, First Lady Jacqueline Kennedy and Texas Governor John Connally got into an open limousine that would take them through the city. As the motorcade passed the downtown Texas School Book Depository building, shots rang out, hitting the President and Governor Connally. Not long after he was rushed to a nearby hospital, President Kennedy was pronounced dead (Connally survived).

Twenty-four-year-old Lee Harvey Oswald was quickly arrested and charged with the killing but never stood trial, since he himself was later gunned down by nightclub owner Jack Ruby—a shooting that was caught by television cameras as it happened. Controversy as to whether Oswald acted alone or as part of a conspiracy has shrouded the JFK assassination ever since.

Newly sworn-in President Lyndon Johnson declared November 24 a national day of mourning. Millions watching the events unfold on television grieved as they took in the heartbreaking coverage of Kennedy's casket being taken to lie in state at the Capitol and, later, of the widowed first lady and her fatherless children viewing the funeral procession.

The Tokens

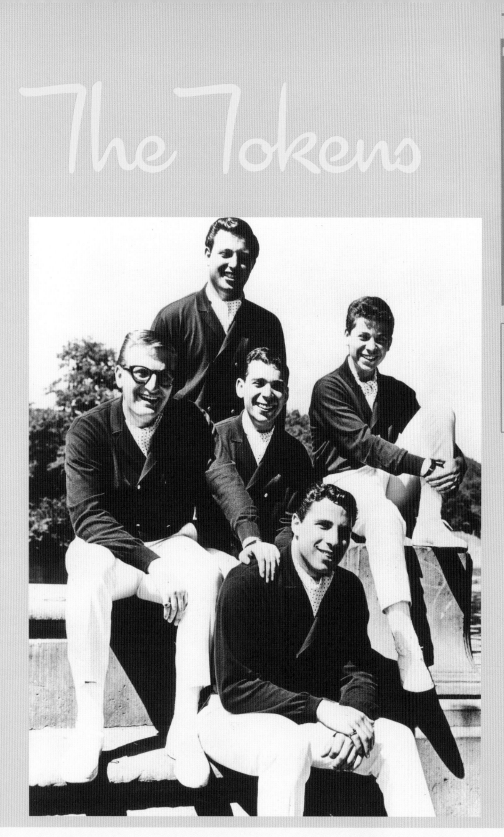

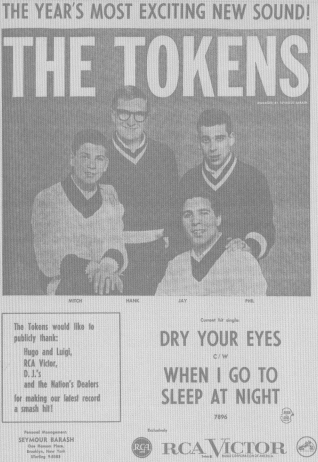

F ormed in the 1950s, the Tokens were originally called the Linc-Tones after their local Brooklyn, New York, high school. Founding member Neil Sedaka sang lead before leaving the group to go on to an extremely successful solo career. The Tokens carried on and recorded the monster hit "The Lion Sleeps Tonight" in 1961.

management huddled their staff behind closed doors and handed out memos:

Effective immediately—No record, information or plug will be aired on this radio station without the express permission of the Program Director.

As bad as payola was, taking the freedom of song selection away from jocks signaled the end of a dream. After all, who was closer to the people than the deejays, who hosted the dance hops, took listener requests, hand-picked the records and interviewed the heroes? But the trust between audiences and on-air personalities had been broken. Remember, this was all happening against a backdrop of increasing skepticism about authority and our nation's traditional institutions. Listeners had trusted deejays to be their bridge to the music that filled their hearts and their lives. They had no idea that the bridge wasn't going to take them all the way across.

It was the beginning of the demise of creativity in radio. Because they feared the Federal Trade Commission and the Federal Communications Commission could shut down a station, general managers at radio stations stifled the deejays and ordered the program directors (PDs) to start controlling the playlists. Rather than nurturing hits from the grassroots artists or trusting the ears of a hit-picking jock, the PD's were only going to allow songs that were already proven hits.

The PDs would base playlists on national charts, like those printed in Billboard, and pretty soon everyone was spinning the same handful of

Little Caesar and the Romans

This quintet from Los Angeles went through a number of name changes but eventually discovered that all roads probably lead to Rome. Their big hit was 1961's "Those Oldies but Goodies (Remind Me of You)."

If doo wop was going to stay off the endangered list, some changes would have to be made and fast.

songs. Programming sameness may have been safe in terms of business, but artistically it was a nightmare, and in my view it ruined radio. It destroyed the capability of people who really were honest and legitimate from exposing product they knew the audience wanted to hear. On the broadest scale, we were nationalizing, which prohibited local and regional artists from ever gaining a foothold in a larger market. The kitchen companies and small labels literally and figuratively lost their "air"—now it was all going to be sucked up by major artists on major labels with major sales receipts.

No one would be listening to the streets and schoolyards where doo wop music was born and raised. Young artists with stars in their eyes and songs on their lips would have nowhere to go.

Prior to the whole payola mess, there was an unspoken promise between the music industry and fans that artists would rise to the top based on the strength of their music. It would be a long time before the music industry would recover its innocence or the faith of listeners. In fact, I don't think it ever has.

Re-evolution

Adapt or perish—that's the unforgiving rule of natural evolution. Musical evolution is the same way, and its history is littered with artists and styles that slipped away into extinction. If doo wop was going to stay off the endangered list, some changes would have to be made, and fast. Doo wop was doubly challenged: At the same time as it had to adapt to a more pop/rock

The Edsels

Word to the wise: If you're going to name your group after a car, don't choose the most infamous failure in automotive history. In fairness, though, the Edsels formed before the Ford flopped. Their hit "Rama Lama Ding Dong," which had been erroneously released under the name "Lama Rama Ding Dong" in 1958, first gained attention after a New York disc jockey realized that it segued perfectly out of "Blue Moon," a huge hit by the Marcels.

Meanwhile, over at Motown...

Berry Gordy Jr. was a twenty-nine-year-old songwriter in 1959 when he launched his record company (at first called Tamla) on the strength of the single "Reet Petite" he wrote for Jackie Wilson and an $800 family loan. The label set up shop in a two-story house in Detroit, Michigan, with a recording studio in the basement and a sign out front reading "Hitsville U.S.A." In 1961, just two years along, Motown had its first #1 R&B hit with the Miracles'"Shop Around" and its first #1 pop hit with the Marvelettes'"Please Mr. Postman." That same year, Gordy signed the Supremes, Stevie Wonder and the Temptations. How's that for a good start?

Establishing a crossover between R&B and pop was central to Gordy's mission. Under his watchful eye, the label thrived with an incredible roster of artists; a crack production team in Lamont Dozier and Eddie and Brian Holland (known as Holland/Dozier/Holland); and a house band known as the Funk Brothers who were central to establishing "the Motown sound." For years, the indie Motown label achieved what so few record companies could: maintaining credibility while exploding on the charts.

Gordy had the vision to foresee a little further up the road, where youth, R&B and pop all crossed paths, and established a business right at the intersection. "The Sound of Young America" lives on in records by Smokey Robinson and the Miracles, Mary Wells, Martha and the Vandellas, the Four Tops, the Isley Brothers, Marvin Gaye, the Jackson 5 and many more.

BERRY GORDY JR.

THE PENTAGONS

ood representatives of the west coast doo wop sound, the Pentagons scored with "To Be Loved (Forever)" and "I Wonder," both released in 1961. Very popular at local hops, both songs spoke to their teenage listeners.

sound to connect with major labels and broad listenerships, the songwriting and delivery would also have to venture further than the three- and four-chord wonders that had guaranteed success just a year before.

A bunch of groups managed the new challenge surprisingly well, and in tandem they made for a second wave of doo wop—a poppier, hipper doo wop. Between 1960 and 1963, the new-wop sound (to coin a phrase) included major hits by the Del-Vikings ("Come Go with Me"), the Earls ("Remember Then"), Shep and the Limelites ("Daddy's Home"), the Marcels ("Heartaches," "Blue Moon"), the Tokens ("The Lion Sleeps Tonight"), the Capris ("There's a Moon Out Tonight") and Bob B. Soxx and the Blue Jeans with their version of "Zip-A-Dee-Doo-Dah," originally from the motion picture *Song of the South*.

Another way to stand out was to step out, but just a handful of vocalists had the goods to go solo in rock 'n' roll-star style. Clyde McPhatter, Ben E. King, Neil Sedaka and Sam Cooke had all passed through doo wop's ranks, and they performed brilliantly as solo artists. Dion DiMucci, formerly with the Belmonts, backed himself up with the Del-Satins and had an enviable run of pop-rock smashes with "Runaround Sue," "The Wanderer," "Little Diane," "Ruby Baby" and "Donna the Prima Donna."

Girl groups blossomed throughout these few years, too, in part because they matched the criteria of the day: Be poppy and look good doing it. The Chantels, the Chiffons and the Bobbettes all came into their own, and none more so than the Shirelles. The Jersey sweethearts had already made their

Doo wop was nice music. Being soft, safe and familiar had helped send the style to the very top in 1958, but now the fans wanted a whole lotta shakin' going on.

Gladys Knight and the Pips

There are few better examples of doo wop's influence put to profoundly good use. Led by a true Georgia peach, the family group Gladys Knight and the Pips have been shining stars of soul for half a century now. They first emerged in 1961 with "Every Beat of My Heart," then sparked a long string of hits by covering Marvin Gaye's "I Heard it Through the Grapevine."

From the early days straight through mega-hits like "Midnight Train to Georgia," "Neither One of Us (Wants to Be the First to Say Goodbye)" and "Best Thing That Ever Happened to Me," we hear in this group a rare balance: heartfelt, gut-wrenching soul, dressed to the nines and delivered with unparalled skill and class.

The Volumes

A pre-Motown act from Detroit, Michigan, the Volumes used to cross over into Canada to sing at local clubs. Their one big hit "I Love You" turned up the volume and climbed up the charts.

RONNIE AND THE HI-LITES

Like many doo wop acts, these Jersey boys met in a church choir. They had one major hit: "I Wish That We Were Married," a tearful teenage lament song.

mark in the late '50s, but they owned 1961 with three giant hits: "Dedicated to the One I Love," "Will You Love Me Tomorrow," and "Mama Said." Banner years followed in '62 and '63 with "Soldier Boy," "Baby It's You" and "Foolish Little Girl."

For the purists of doo wop, though, times were not quite so rosy. Those who sustained any career at all had retreated to regional markets, where their yesteryear hits might still get spun on local stations or help them fill seats at a town theater. Their love for tradition deserves respect, but performing doo wop as it had been heard in its former glory was a surefire way of branding an "oldies" group, with oldie fans to boot. Artists who could strike the delicate balance between 1960s tastes and 1950s songsmithing were one in a million. And the one that comes to mind is the unsinkable Drifters. They topped the charts several times between 1960 and 1963 with greats like "This Magic Moment," "Save the Last Dance for Me," "Please Stay," "Some Kind of Wonderful," "Up on the Roof" and "On Broadway." The Drifters were masters of change, and they managed to maintain the best qualities of doo wop while incorporating it into any number of passing styles over their four-decade career. But they were a rare talent. Other than the Drifters, doo wop in its purest form had been shoved into a time capsule, and the door was slamming shut.

At a time when pop culture wanted everything to be fresh and new, holding on to old ways of making music or doing business was fatal. Tastes had changed—what was once charming was now quaint. And we'd seen the cracks in authority, which had proven its capacity for deceit.

The doo wop artists who made it through the early 1960s had been wise to adapt. It was the only way to survive, and they managed to breathe a few more years of life into their careers. But by taking on more elements of rock 'n' roll, pop and the emerging R&B sound, doo wop had evolved right out of its own skin.

> *The doo wop artists who made it through the early 1960s had been wise to adapt. It was the only way to survive.*

GREGORY PECK, IN THE OSCAR-WINNING ROLE OF ATTICUS FINCH, DEFENDS TOM ROBINSON, PLAYED BY BROOK PETERS

To Kill A Mockingbird

Harper Lee's magnificent book from 1960 was a coming-of-age story—not just for young Scout Finch and her brother, Jem, but for America. As the Finch kids are learning not to prejudge a mysterious character on their block, their entire hometown is indulging preconceptions about a black man accused of raping a white woman. Even the virtuous Atticus Finch, their attorney father, can't keep poor Tom Robinson from the malicious intentions of hateful people.

Set in 1930s Alabama, *To Kill A Mockingbird* asked us to re-examine our conscience and consider the moral fate of our children. "If there's just one kind of folks," Jem asks, "why can't they get along with each other?"

A one-hit wonder from Bakersfield, California, the Paradons' "Diamonds and Pearls" sparked the imagination of teenagers across the country.

THE SAFARIS

One-hit wonders from Los Angeles, the Safaris scored with their debut song "Image of a Girl." A quintessential summer song, "Image" made all landlocked listeners long for the surf and all surfers want to be landlocked with someone special.

Kathy Young and the Innocents

California teenage pop singer Kathy Young met the Innocents at a television taping and good vibes followed. The Innocents already had a hit with 1960's "Honest I Do" and another when they sang backup for Kathy on her top-selling record "A Thousand Stars."

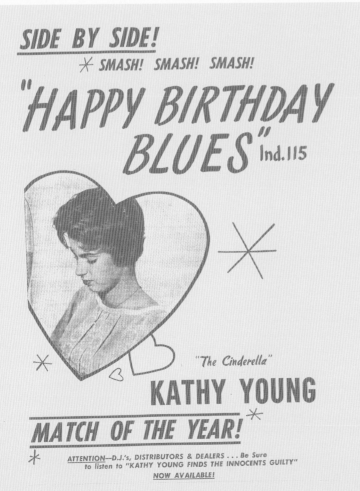

SIDE BY SIDE!
✱ SMASH! SMASH! SMASH!
"HAPPY BIRTHDAY BLUES" Ind. 115

"The Cinderella"
KATHY YOUNG
MATCH OF THE YEAR!

ATTENTION—D.J.'s, DISTRIBUTORS & DEALERS . . . Be Sure to listen to "KATHY YOUNG FINDS THE INNOCENTS GUILTY" NOW AVAILABLE!

THE VALENTINOS

Sam Cooke discovered this gospel-singing group of brothers from Cleveland and signed them to his SAR Records company. They had one hit, "Looking for a Love."

The Chanters

Schoolboy doo wop, best exemplified by Frankie Lymon and the Teenagers, had proven the appeal of kids singing for kids. The Chanters worked a similar formula with "My My Darling" in 1958, though the song was never heard far beyond their New York hometown. Another song they had recorded in 1958, "No, No, No," had a strong run three years later—but by the time it reached national airwaves in 1961, the group had broken up.

THE SHELLS

Brooklyn boys who recorded "Baby Oh Baby" in the late 1950s, the Shells struck twice and cracked the Top 40 in 1960 with its high-profile reissue.

The Corsairs

After the three Uzell brothers—Jay, James and Moses—teamed with cousin George Wooten, they headed north from their North Carolina home to seek their fortune. Other than 1962's "Smokey Places," the Corsairs are nearly lost to the ages, but they helped provide an invaluable stepping stone between doo wop and Motown-era R&B.

SMOKY PLACES
(Abner Spector)

TUFF

THE CORSAIRS
Personal Manager
Abner Spector

a Tuff
Record Artist

Exclu-Agency
Universal Attractions
200 W. 57th Street
New York 19, N.Y.

THE VIBRATIONS

Originally called the Jayhawks when they formed in Los Angeles in the 1950s, the Vibrations recorded feel-good music like "The Watusi" in 1961 and later "My Girl Sloopy."

Randy and the Rainbows

Hailing from Queens, New York, Dominick "Randy" Safuto and brother Frank spent some time as The Dialtones before being renamed the Rainbows. Latecomers to the doo wop era, their big 1963 hit "Denise" is considered a favorite to this day.

THE EARLS

The heart of rock 'n' roll was beating in this doo wop group from the Bronx, New York. Larry Chance and his group hit in 1961 with "Life Is But a Dream" and a year later with "Remember Then."

THE CAPRIS

The Capris hailed from New York City and were an all-Italian doo wop group, which begs the question: Did they name themselves for the Ford Lincoln Capri, or the Italian island of Capri? "There's a Moon Out Tonight" was their big hit in 1958, allowing them to eclipse the Philadelphia group of the same name—even though the Philly Capris had formed several years earlier. By pure coincidence, both groups had also penned tunes called "God Only Knows."

The Duprees

Originally calling themselves the Parisiennes, this quintet was able to hold on to their French flair when the Coed label asked the boys to change their name. Many doo wop artists have mined hits of old, and the Duprees had the good taste to recreate chart success in 1962 by covering Joe Stafford's hit "You Belong to Me" from ten years before.

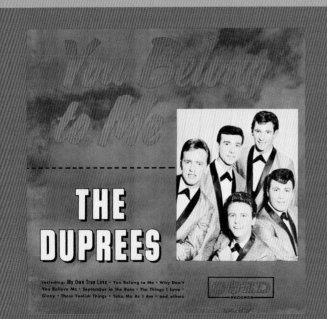

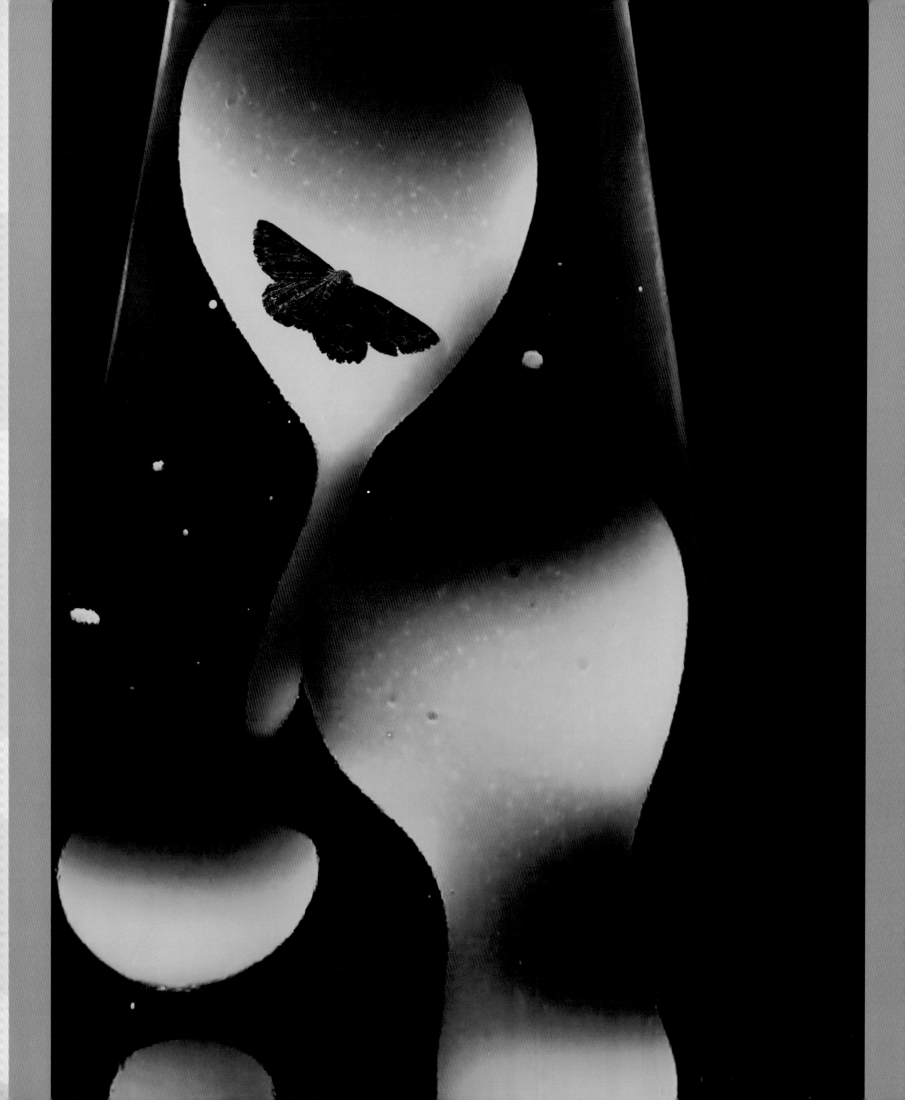

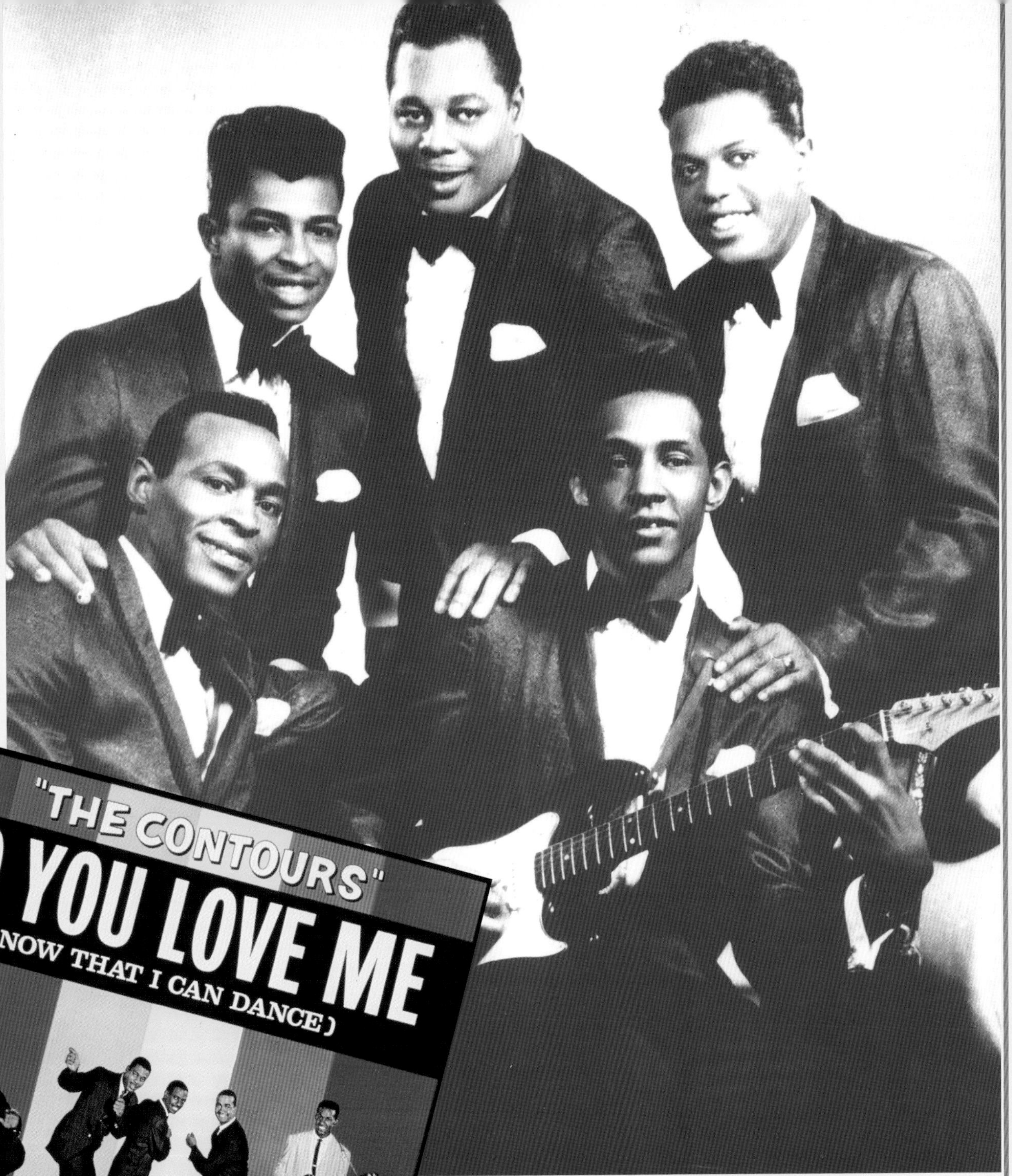

"THE CONTOURS"
DO YOU LOVE ME
(NOW THAT I CAN DANCE)

SHAKE SHERRIE

FIRST I LOOK AT THE PURSE
CAN YOU JERK LIKE ME

DO YOU LOVE ME   WHOLE LOTTA WOMAN

The Contours

D o You Love Me" was a fun-spirited dance hit in 1962, and was delivered with a rock 'n' roll rasp that had less in common with doo wop past than R&B to come. The Contours' hit enjoyed a revival in 1987 thanks to the movie *Dirty Dancing*, which was set in 1962. That happens to be one of my favorite movies, by the way. I play the magician who saws Baby in half!

THE CAPRIS

The Capris hailed from New York City and were an all-Italian doo wop group, which begs the question: Did they name themselves for the Ford Lincoln Capri, or the Italian island of Capri? "There's a Moon Out Tonight" was their big hit in 1958, allowing them to eclipse the Philadelphia group of the same name—even though the Philly Capris had formed several years earlier. By pure coincidence, both groups had also penned tunes called "God Only Knows."

The Duprees

Originally calling themselves the Parisiennes, this quintet was able to hold on to their French flair when the Coed label asked the boys to change their name. Many doo wop artists have mined hits of old, and the Duprees had the good taste to recreate chart success in 1962 by covering Joe Stafford's hit "You Belong to Me" from ten years before.

THE JARMELS

N o institution reared more rhythm and blues talent than the church, and the Jarmels are yet another fine example. A southern group looking for a glint of city glitter, the Jarmels were from Richmond, Virginia, but named themselves after a street in Harlem. In their heartbroken but very clean hit "A Little Bit of Soap," the singer cries that he can scrub off his girlfriend's lipstick, powder and perfume, but "never wash away my tears."

CHAPTER 7
1964–1966

Doo Wop, Soul, and the Future of Rock 'n' Roll

Popular music is a simple pleasure—we use it to dance, to romance, to get into a trance. But any one song is really the result of a very complex structure that is impacted by a huge number of factors. It's like a painting that appears uncomplicated but actually has twenty layers of paint on the canvas. We've been scraping away at those layers here as we consider the palette of social, financial, technological and political colors that helped create the doo wop picture.

By the end of 1963, the sun had set on doo wop's glory days; that much is fair to say. The pop and R&B charts of 1964 featured just a few rare birds, like the Drifters with "Under the Boardwalk" and…and…well, that was about it! However—and this point is central to my message—doo wop didn't die. Just as it hadn't appeared from out of nowhere, it wasn't about to simply blink out of existence. It was painted over, but the colors bled through, adding depth and texture to the work of new artists.

So, doo wop did not come to an end. Rather, it was absorbed. Anyone with an appreciation for infectious vocal harmonies and innocent melodies could hear it, sometimes subtly and

Doo wop was painted over, but the colors bled through, adding depth to the work of new artists.

sometimes blatantly, in the rhythm & blues, soul, folk and many splinterings of rock 'n' roll that came long after classic doo wop had fallen off of most people's radar.

Meet the Beatles

The Beatles ruled in 1964. Never before had one act captured all Top 5 slots of the best-selling singles chart (as they did in the first week of April '64) or the love of so many teenagers. For a year there had been loud rumblings from across the Atlantic about these four mop-tops, even before the _Please Please Me_ long-player was released in the U.K. Taking nothing away from the singular appeal and genius of the Beatles, it's worth noting that this first release was nearly half cover tunes; even the Beatles were links in the long chain of popular music, and they capitalized on the past before connecting us to the future. Two songs from _Please Please Me_ were straight out of doo wop, too, and both had already been made famous by the Shirelles. "Boys," a girly love song sung tongue-in-cheek by Ringo Starr, had been the successful flip side of 1960's "Will You Love Me Tomorrow," and the girls had taken "Baby It's You" to #8 in 1961. The Fab Four paid tribute to their vocal heroes, doo wop greats among them, on dozens of sides throughout their career.

Clearly, Beatlemania transformed the music and the pop culture of the 1960s. They also ushered in the first British Invasion, a wave of U.K. artists who had been affected and infected by stateside rock 'n' roll and who flocked to America in the mid-1960s. The Hollies, the Bee Gees, Dusty

THE RICH VOCAL HARMONIES OF BOTH PETER, PAUL & MARY AND SIMON & GARFUNKEL HAVE THEIR ROOTS IN DOO WOP.

THE BEATLES
ARRIVE IN AMERICA

> *The city never has witnessed the excitement that's been stirred by these youngsters from Liverpool who call themselves the Beatles...*
> —Ed Sullivan

Ed Sullivan's words were no understatement, and New York's reaction to the Beatles' arrival would soon be mirrored across the nation. The appearance of the Fab Four on his television show sparked the Beatlemania that first swept America in 1964.

I was there on February 7 when the Beatles landed at John F. Kennedy International Airport (JFK) in New York. They came in on Pan American Flight 101—I'll never forget it. The kids were going nuts, just screaming their heads off, and the girls were reaching and grabbing at the group. Some fans held funny signs that read "The Beatles are starving our barbers" and "Beatles unfair to bald men"! There was a brief press conference at a makeshift setup in the Pan American terminal, and the Beatles seemed a little nervous in front of the American reporters. The press hadn't been so nice to the Beatles, after all, and were looking for some dirt. They asked questions like, "Are you going to get a haircut at all?" George Harrison responded, "I had one yesterday" and got a big laugh.

NEW

THE FAB FOUR COME BACK

BEATLES

PDC
35¢

4 WONDERFUL COLOR PIN-UPS

100S OF EXCLUSIVE PICTURES

Ideal
MAGAZINE

WIVES THEY HIDE ★ GIRLS THEY WANT

FEUDS: ROLLING STONES
DAVE CLARK 5 **WIN RINGO'S RINGS**

The mad scene at the airport made for great publicity, but in truth much of it had been orchestrated. The group's manager, Brian Epstein, was a sharp businessman and would not bring the Beatles to the U.S. until they already had a #1 record. He wanted the riots and the madhouse response. I think it's important to note that without a serious dose of hype and publicity, Beatlemania would never have happened. We know now that the group was extraordinarily talented, but at the time they had only released a handful of pop songs. The hype machine, greased by record companies, radio stations and the Beatles themselves, played a major role in kick-starting Beatlemania.

New York City was electrified. On the first night they played *The Ed Sullivan Show*, I was covering the scene for WABC radio (which we had taken to calling "W-A-Beatle-C"). That night, outside the theater it was like New Year's Eve—a real wild happening. They say there wasn't one teenage incident reported in the entire United States that night because all the kids were home watching the Beatles on TV!

It was even crazier at the Warwick Hotel where the group was staying. I was broadcasting live from there, and I saw girls hiding in hampers full of dirty linens to get a glimpse of John, Paul, George or Ringo. Some of the kids were riding on top of the elevators. Outside there must have been five thousand of them listening on transistor radios and waiting for the Beatles to roll up. We were all looking for their limo—I remember hanging out of a window with a colleague holding on to the seat of my pants as I broadcasted from the eighth floor. When a Bentley limousine pulled up, the crowd surged and pushed through the police barrier. I saw a police horse go down. But instead of the Beatles a group called the Teddy Boys, attempting to cash in on the hysteria with a publicity stunt, got out of the Bentley. Soon the kids were back under control,

though not for long. The Beatles were making their way west on 54th Street, the wrong way on a one-way street, with a police escort. It was complete pandemonium when they tried to get into the hotel. You know, I think the Teddy Boys are still locked up in the basement of the Warwick.

Beatlemania was youth-driven but would have been stifled without some sort of tacit acceptance by parents. Ed Sullivan paved the way for their approval when he described the Beatles on air as "nice young men." *The Ed Sullivan Show* was a family institution at the time, having been accepted into every American household. So when he gave the Beatles his stamp of approval, parents knew their kids weren't going to go to the devil.

Another trusted broadcaster had played a behind-the-scenes role. When Sullivan was first deciding whether to book the Beatles, he called Walter Cronkite to inquire if he'd heard of the young Brits. When Cronkite asked his young daughter in the next room "Ever heard of the Beatles?" Sullivan could hear her scream in glee. When you think about it, this little girl helped the Beatles score their most pivotal gig. Cronkite made sure she had a seat at the show, too.

About a week after the Ed Sullivan performances (they played three times: twice in New York and once on a special broadcast from Miami), my listeners all developed British accents. A caller phoning in a request would say, "Eh, Sir Brucie, would you mind playing a record for me and me bird?" Kids dressed like them, got the Prince Valiant haircuts, and tried to speak like they were from Liverpool.

When you get a group that can affect even our language, you know you have something very special. Culturally, everybody was identifying so closely with these guys. We had been looking for something; in the wake of intense political tension, the assassinations and racial strife, we were in dire need of some fun. The Beatles brought it to us on a solid gold platter.

If there was one group carrying the doo wop torch, it was the Beach Boys.

Springfield, the Zombies, the Moody Blues and many more showed a keen appreciation for vocal harmony, and some of their greatest hits are woven through with the influence of doo wop.

It wasn't entirely unusual for a traditional doo wop act to make a chart appearance now and then in the mid-1960s (the Platters, Little Anthony and the Imperials, Jay and the Americans), but far more familiar to the high life were their domestic rock and pop offspring. Jan and Dean, the Righteous Brothers, the Four Seasons, the Four Tops, the Shangri-Las and the Byrds all owed a doo wop debt, but if there was one group carrying the torch to the new generation, it was the Beach Boys. Cruisin' with the ease and laid-back vocal style introduced by the Robins and the Platters before them, the Beach Boys were definitively West Coast. They stripped away some of doo wop's dated characteristics like the comically low bass and the precise midrange articulations, but still much of their catalog sounds like doo wop on vacation, bathed in sunshine. Unlike so many of their contemporaries—though very much like their doo wop forefathers—the Beach Boys kept their lyrics limited to girls, sun, cars and fun.

There was a place for fun and light-hearted messages in pop music, but an emphasis on social and political change was beginning to pervade the teenage mindset. It was no more avoidable than the dark clouds of mistrust and fear that rained down on us with assassinations, wars and fork-tongued politicians. We struggled for civil rights, women's rights and sexual liberation. It was also a thrilling time, and we quite literally shot for the moon. We learned that youthful visions were not a lark—we really did have the power to change things for the better. Music played a dual role through all of this. It was, as it had always been, a relieving dose of escapism. At the same time, rock 'n' roll was gaining a conscience.

Step back in time for a minute here and consider what a different environment this was from the era in which doo wop matured. The innocent turns of phrase, the funny bass singers, the kitchen companies—none of it could have survived the '60s and, more to the point, it would never have been born in that environment. As the Byrds sang in 1965, "Turn, turn, turn," doo wop had its purpose and its season. Again, music is the reflection of its time.

Folk for all folks

Mirroring the social scene of the 1960s, by contrast, was a generation of conscientious singer/songwriters who were celebrated as the poets of their generation. With his first three records released in the early 1960s, Bob Dylan became the leader of a clan of pacifist rebels— plenty of them in the audience, and many onstage such as Joan Baez, Joni Mitchell and Pete Seeger. Now the voice of youth was not singing about doing the Twist or making out at the submarine races. This was music with a message, delivered by colorful personalities whose music was married to their image.

As organic and acoustically driven as Dylan and company were (at least initially), this age of icons benefited from the reach of technology. We knew

Rock 'n' roll was gaining a social conscience.

"SHINDIG!" and "HULLABALOO" Debut

While *American Bandstand* was already an afternoon TV institution by the mid-1960s, there were two other nationally airing shows that dominated the teen-dance market: *Shindig!* and *Hullabaloo.*

Shindig!, telecast in black and white, was hosted by Los Angeles deejay Jimmy O'Neill and ran on ABC from 1964 to 1966. Putting loud rock 'n' roll and wild dancing on primetime TV was a risky move in the days when the quaint *Andy Griffith Show* ruled the airwaves. But *Shindig!* was a smash. Youthful viewers tuned in weekly to watch up-and-coming and chart-topping acts like Chuck Berry, the Beatles and others play their current hits for an audience of screaming teens. In addition to featuring the biggest stars and the newest dances, *Shindig!* helped break down cultural barriers by showing racially diverse artists, dancers and audiences simply having a great time together.

With the success of *Shindig!* came NBC takeoff *Hullabaloo*, which aired from 1965 to 1966. Unlike the show that inspired it, *Hullabaloo* was presented in full, glorious color from the start and boasted a different guest host every week; emceeing stars like Frankie Avalon and Petula Clark would sing a couple of their own songs and introduce the other acts. The Hullabaloo Dancers kept everything moving, sometimes with featured artists like the Rolling Stones or the Supremes. For the Top Pop Medley, the host and some of the guests would get together for brief renditions of whatever was hot on the charts, while the last song of each episode was usually shot on a mod nightclub set called the Hullabaloo A Go-Go. Groovy, man!

Besides being popular, fun shows full of great music and non-stop dancing, *Shindig!* and *Hullabaloo* demonstrated the importance of the youth market to the networks. And they reminded everyone watching at home that, yes, it really was okay to be young.

The Temptations

The Temptations were the sultans of smooth, and the only thing more polished than their dancing shoes were their fine, fluent harmonies. The group featured a round-robin of soulful lead vocalists, but the man primarily responsible for their phenomenal success wasn't even in the band.

Smokey Robinson, working for Motown Records while pursuing his career as a performer, wrote and produced the Temptations' most enduring hits. "The Way You Do the Things You Do," "My Girl," "Since I Lost My Baby" and "Get Ready" all came from Smokey's pen and capitalized on the Tempts' broad skill set. The group took a turn for the funky late in the '60s, a decided departure from their founding sound. Incidentally, the Temptations were earlier known as the Primes. They had a crosstown sister band in Detroit called the Primettes—who became the Supremes.

SN 66023

THE BEACH BOYS

Both the music and the spirit of doo wop is traceable in the Beach Boys, who may be the most celebrated vocal group in all of pop music. The sun-lovin' Beach Boys had quite a few doo wop characteristics, in fact. They were a family group at heart, having been started by the three Wilson brothers (Brian, Dennis and Carl), a cousin (Mike Love) and a friend from school (Al Jardine). They were also a family business, with the brothers' father, Murray Wilson, initially taking the reins as producer and manager until his boys had a record deal.

The group broke Billboard's Hot 100 in 1962 with "Surfin'," and they soon rode a wave of hits based on the stellar songwriting chops of Brian Wilson. Brian had found early inspiration in the novel jazz harmonies of the Four Freshmen, just as doo wop groups like the Harptones had. Hits like "Good Vibrations,""Little Deuce Coupe" and "Fun, Fun, Fun" echo the Beach Boys' wholesome themes of love, cruising in cars and good times with good girls. While the Beach Boys' lyrical load was typically light, 1966's *Pet Sounds* is one of the most highly acclaimed releases in all of pop and rock, and it's probably the first concept album ever. Brian Wilson felt stiff competition with the Beatles, but Paul McCartney himself has been quoted as saying,"It was *Pet Sounds* that blew me out of the water."

Like so many of the artists in these pages, a tide of nostalgia restored the Beach Boys' earlier success. *Endless Summer*, a double-album released in 1974, was comprised entirely of material from 1963–1966, but that didn't stop it from hitting #1 and selling millions of copies.

THE VIETNAM WAR

The Vietnam War era was one of the most turbulent periods in America's twentieth century history, and also one of the saddest. Night after night on the evening news we saw the terrible images of death and destruction and heard the day's body counts. We watched report upon report of the growing civil unrest here at home, as hippies took to the streets to protest the draft and what they saw as a horribly unjust war.

America's direct involvement in Vietnam started after the Gulf of Tonkin incident involving U.S. warships in 1964, when the U.S. began escalating its military commitment and sending troops to help the South Vietnamese against the communist-backed North Vietnamese rebels. The situation became a horrible quagmire as more and more young American men were drafted and sent to fight in a war many didn't always believe in—against an enemy the U.S. had clearly underestimated.

American troop withdrawals began in 1973 but the conflict dragged on until 1975. When the last American soldiers were evacuated from the embassy in April 1975 and South Vietnam surrendered, the war was over at last. Unfortunately, once our troops returned home, they were not all greeted as heroic survivors. They did not receive the respect they deserved. To this day, it is a blot on our American history.

None of us will ever fully understand the Vietnam War and the events that surrounded it. It seems that every few decades in our nation's growth, tragedy arises when leaders try to hold on to the old ways of resolving issues and drag the youth into their plans—a situation that's being repeated today. But, as Marvin Gaye once sang, "War is not the answer."

Bob Dylan

N o one artist can shift the tide of popular music, but Bob Dylan certainly represented a turning point in the '60s. There's a good chance, though, that mass audiences and the culture of Baby Boomers have elevated the importance of Dylan's work to a height that even he might contest. Dylan's socially conscious folk songs of the early 1960s made him a rallying point for the frustrations, fears and newfound freedoms of the era's young people. He's to be admired for reinventing himself ("Don't look back" apparently being a personal motto) several times in his career, regardless of fan support. As a songwriter whose lyrics have been analyzed as literary works, and an icon revered as "the spokesman of a generation," he also deserves credit for reportedly handing the title of "America's greatest living poet" over to Smokey Robinson!

The Supremes

All the pieces of the puzzle were there at the beginning of the Supremes' career—they just had to be put in the right place. After a few false starts, Berry Gordy, who had signed the female quartet to his Motown label, shifted Diana Ross to lead vocals. He also assigned the group to his famed writing/production team of Brian Holland, Lamont Dozier and Eddie Holland, who gave the girls their first #1 hit in 1964 with "Where Did Our Love Go." A long string of timeless hits, many by Holland/Dozier/Holland, followed in the years to come, including "Baby Love,""Stop! In the Name of Love" and "I Hear a Symphony." Need more superlatives? The Supremes were not just the best-selling girl group but the best-selling African American group of the 1960s. They had twelve #1 hits between 1964 and 1969, including a record-breaking streak of five consecutive #1's in 1965.

who Dylan was—how he dressed, what his political beliefs were—just as well as we knew his melodies, thanks to the exposure afforded him by television, syndicated radio and the well-oiled distribution mechanisms of the music industry. These artists may have pushed hard against the establishment, but the cogs were in place to turn the gears of business, marketing and promotion that made them heroes. Exponentially more than in the decade prior, technology accelerated their connection to young audiences and the youth's relevance to the mainstream.

A cadre of other folk-inflected artists swept into the fold, many of them more in the tradition of vocal group harmony than Dylan ever allowed in his one-man show (in which he made a conscious decision to shun vocal technique). This group featured a range of folk influences: There were traditionalists like the Kingston Trio, Peter, Paul and Mary, and the Highwaymen; and then artists like the Mamas and the Papas and Simon and Garfunkel who shared as much in common with pop as they did with hallowed doo wop harmony.

Don't forget the Motor City

Nowhere was the legacy of doo wop more alive than in the rhythm & blues of Motown Records. At the helm of the Motown label (named for its "Motor City" home of Detroit, Michigan), Berry Gordy Jr. established a link between the gospel, blues and soul of the past and the R&B of the future. Doo wop's blood had been thinned in the rock and pop veins; in Motown, it ran thick.

Diana Ross and the Supremes were cut from the Shirelles' cloth.

PATTI LABELLE AND THE BLUE BELLES

Originally known simply as the Blue Belles, this Philadelphia girl group had a pop/R&B crossover hit in 1962 with "I Sold My Heart to the Junkman" (recorded four years earlier by the Silhouettes). Right about that time, Ms. Patricia Holt changed her name to Patti LaBelle, making it clear as a bell that she was dedicating her life to her music. The group had five more R&B hits between 1962 and 1967; don't miss "Down the Aisle," the 1963 hit in which Patti shows off her amazing vocal range. To this day she is forever achieving new heights as a vocalist, even as fans call again and again for her 1975 #1 hit, "Lady Marmalade."

Fashion Revolutions

TWIGGY

The mid-1960s brought revolutions in many areas, waves of new ideas in politics, social attitudes, art, film, theater and music. But there was yet another domain that saw numerous exciting changes back then: the world of fashion.

And if there's one garment that comes to mind when discussing '60s fashion, it's the mini skirt. Commonly credited to English designer Mary Quant, the mini skirt's raised hemline (a scandalous eight inches above the knees!) raised eyebrows, body temperatures and, in some cases, tempers, around the world when Quant began marketing it in 1965. Quant and her fellow designers opened hip boutiques on Kings Road and Carnaby Street in London's Chelsea district to sell their sleek, colorful new "mod" (short for modernist) designs. Wearing the latest offerings, stick-thin supermodel Twiggy epitomized the "Swinging London" look.

At last there was something new to look at in the world of fashion. Compared to the more restrictive, still-lingering styles of the 1940s and '50s, the mini skirt and other fashion innovations were a feast for the eyes. These new designs reflected youth and were perfect for teenagers and young adult women—and for their moms who wanted to look and feel younger. In a decade of fast-moving change, the mini skirt was a garment that said, "Let's get on with the future."

The Miracles

Having been formed in the mid-1950's, this singing quintet could not help but have a heavy doo wop influence: William "Smokey" Robinson had been inspired by Nolan Strong and his group the Diablos, who were also from Detroit, and in their early days the Miracles were turned down for sounding too much like the Platters. They also first attracted label attention with "Got a Job," an "answer" record to the Silhouettes' hit "Get a Job."

If music legend has it right, it was Smokey Robinson who suggested Berry Gordy Jr. start his own label—and since the Miracles were Gordy's first signing to what would become Motown Records, his motivation seems pretty clear! But Smokey made good, and then some. Even before he became a creative tour de force at the label, he led the Miracles up the charts in 1960 with "Shop Around." The Miracles were great on mid-tempo numbers like "You've Really Got a Hold On Me" and "The Tracks of My Tears" but it was on ballads like "Ooo Baby Baby" that Smokey was truly miraculous. His sweet falsetto sounds as good today as it did 45 years ago.

Nowhere was the legacy of doo wop more alive than in the rhythm & blues of Motown.

The pioneers of Motown were reared on doo wop, and many of its shining stars even began their careers in doo wop groups. Smokey Robinson not only sang some of Motown's greatest songs but was vice president of the label and in 1957, together with the Miracles, had been Gordy's first find. Smokey was inspired to put his first band together when he heard the Diablos as a kid, and his love of doo wop was influential as he scouted new artists for Motown. Throughout his long career, Smokey has continually explored brilliant new territory, but he's never strayed far from the doo wop formula of stringing a silky lead high over the top of a warm vocal chorus.

Show me an R&B legend and I'll show you a singer who bowed at the altar of doo wop. Ben E. King and Clyde McPhatter had of course each taken a turn leading the Drifters, and Jackie Wilson had replaced McPhatter in Billy Ward and the Dominoes. The amazing Sam Cooke was there at doo wop's genesis with the Soul Stirrers, Marvin Gaye sang for the Moonglows and Wilson Pickett for the Falcons.

Need I go on? Gladys Knight and the Pips were doo wop with a soul injection. Diana Ross and the Supremes were cut from the Shirelles' cloth, and Michael Jackson fronting the Jackson 5 was a fresh take on Frankie Lymon and the Teenagers. The Temptations were also influenced by Frankie Lymon and the Teenagers, as well as the Cadillacs and the Drifters. Back east, Lee Andrews and the Hearts were one of many doo wop groups in

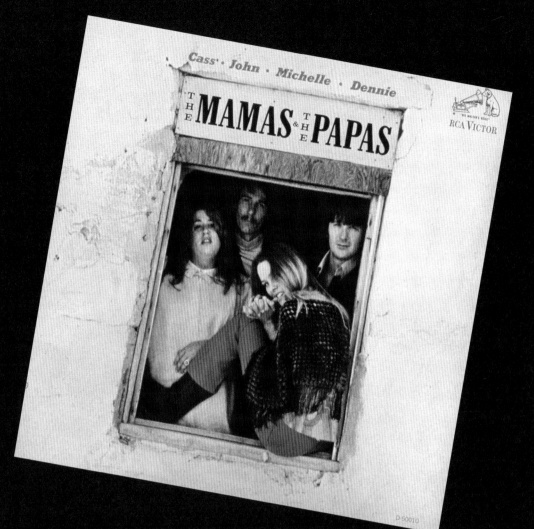

The Mamas and the Papas

This group took vocal harmony on a trip where it had never ventured before. Part folk, part pop and all hippie, the Mamas and the Papas jump-started with "California Dreamin'" as their debut single. Among the hits to follow was a cover of the Shirelles' "Dedicated to the One I Love." While their harmonies were produced with a much grander sound than the bare, minimalist approach of doo wop recordings, "Dedicated" has a spoken intro that is straight out of the doo wop tradition.

Civil Rights and Dr. Martin Luther King

DR. MARTIN LUTHER KING (CENTER) LEADS A PROTEST MARCH

After the McCarthy era showed us we weren't always being told the truth, the next big shock to Americans came in the early and mid-1960s, with the ugly and violent displays of racial intolerance that festered during the peak of the civil rights movement. To those of us living in the cocoons of large, culturally diverse cities, the scenes on TV of racist brutality and of protesters being blasted with fire hoses in parts of the Deep South were a sure sign that all was still not right in much of our country.

The modern African American civil rights movement had kicked off earlier with the landmark Supreme Court ruling in the Brown v. Board of Education case, which made segregation unconstitutional. But in the face of the continued institutionalized prejudice in much of the South, the court's decision had only slowly been enforced. So under the leadership of Dr. Martin Luther King Jr., many activists turned to peaceful methods of civil disobedience: sit-ins, bus boycotts and demonstrations like the 1965 Selma to Montgomery marches. Tragically, we would lose King to an assassin's bullet just three years after the historic Alabama marches.

King was and will always be an inspiring individual, not just to African Americans striving for equality but to people everywhere who value freedom and human dignity. The awareness of racism in America raised by the 1960s civil rights movement represents the most important social development in our nation's recent history. Sadly, the issue of race is one we continue to grapple with today.

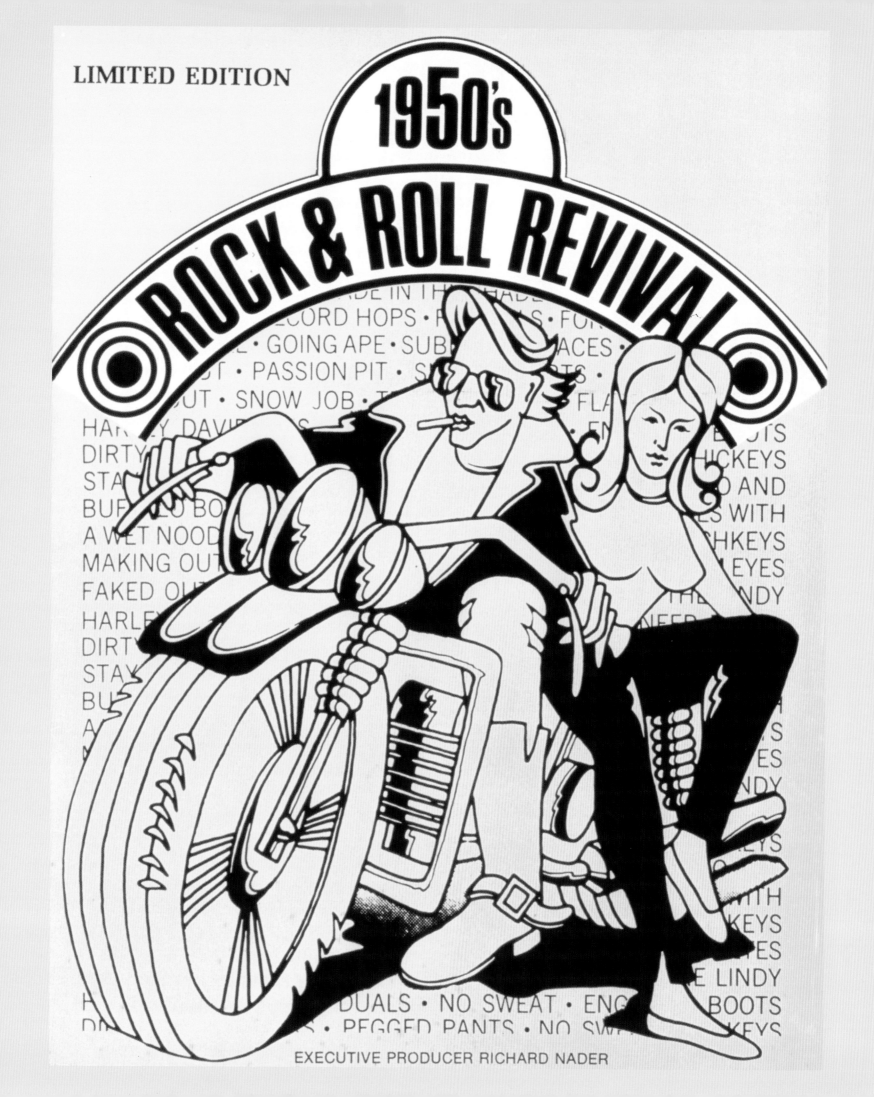

NEW MUSIC, NEW DANCES

DANCERS FROM GET YOURSELF A COLLEGE GIRL

In 1964, America was turned upside down by a musical deluge from across the Atlantic known as "the British Invasion."

The Beatles led the charge, but not far behind were dozens of other longhaired, uniquely clad "beat" groups— the Rolling Stones, the Kinks, the Zombies, the Yardbirds, the Dave Clark Five, Manfred Mann, Herman's Hermits, the Hollies, the Moody Blues and Gerry and the Pacemakers, to name just a few. Between 1964 and 1966, it seemed like almost every hit on the charts was by a hot young English band or solo artist.

And with the new sound came new dances. The twist of the early '60s gave way to the Jerk, the Mule, the Freddie, the Boogaloo and the Frug. And the timing was perfect. By the mid-'60s we were ready to move, to shift gears, get out and have a little fun and exercise, and to smile a little. It helped us to de-stress and get our minds off the serious political and social events that were happening in the world.

Yet another big change in music was right around the corner, as the U.S. west coast (San Francisco, in particular) was about to launch a sweeping new movement of socially conscious, psychedelic protest rock. This music would be less about dancing, more about thinking and "experiencing." But for a couple of years in the mid-'60s, our feet just wouldn't stop moving.

After the McCarthy era showed us we weren't always being told the truth, the next big shock to Americans came in the early and mid-1960s, with the ugly and violent displays of racial intolerance that festered during the peak of the civil rights movement. To those of us living in the cocoons of large, culturally diverse cities, the scenes on TV of racist brutality and of protesters being blasted with fire hoses in parts of the Deep South were a sure sign that all was still not right in much of our country.

The modern African American civil rights movement had kicked off earlier with the landmark Supreme Court ruling in the Brown v. Board of Education case, which made segregation unconstitutional. But in the face of the continued institutionalized prejudice in much of the South, the court's decision had only slowly been enforced. So under the leadership of Dr. Martin Luther King Jr., many activists turned to peaceful methods of civil disobedience: sit-ins, bus boycotts and demonstrations like the 1965 Selma to Montgomery marches. Tragically, we would lose King to an assassin's bullet just three years after the historic Alabama marches.

King was and will always be an inspiring individual, not just to African Americans striving for equality but to people everywhere who value freedom and human dignity. The awareness of racism in America raised by the 1960s civil rights movement represents the most important social development in our nation's recent history. Sadly, the issue of race is one we continue to grapple with today.

DR. MARTIN LUTHER KING (CENTER) LEADS A PROTEST MARCH

What attracted you to the music business?

There was no rock 'n' roll when I grew up, no teenage music. I listened to Hank Williams and Jimmy Reed. But later, hearing groups like the Cadillacs doing "Speedo" was instant identity—it was my music! It was the sound, the approach—a little rebellious, with a sense of urgency.

What do think gives doo wop its timeless appeal?

You didn't need a band or tuxedos. I know that today you see it presented that way, but all you really needed was four or five guys on the corner. It was street music—you didn't need a whole lot. It came from the heart and it gets to the heart.

What are your favorite doo wop songs and groups?

I love the Cleftones and the Dells. I love the Ronettes' "Be My Baby." "Maybe" is one of my favorite songs in the world! "Speedo" by the Cadillacs changed my whole life. The sense of urgency resonated with everything I was going through as a pre-teen. If all those feelings had stayed inside and I had no way to express them, I woulda gotten twisted.

What are your favorite memories of doo wop or the 1950s in general?

Backstage at the Brooklyn Fox, with Chuck Berry, Jerry Lee Lewis, Little Richard, the Everly Brothers, the Ronettes, the Crests—it brought the races together in some way. My best memory is Little Richard's mother telling me, "For a white boy, you have soul— you're part of the family, boy!" It's one of the greatest compliments I ever got.

What do you think is the major difference between the music business today and when you started?

Today the business seems too big to get your arms around. There's a lot of technical advances in equipment that I love, and major differences in transportation, which would have been welcome back in my day. Today, people use synthesizers to create the mood behind your lyrics. But we used vocals—*oohs* and *aahs*. I'm blessed to come from a time when the music was very spontaneous, heartfelt and organic, without a whole lot of formula.

CHAPTER 8

Doo Wop Lovers Never Say Goodbye

Is doo wop still alive? Let me answer that question with a question: Does your heart still beat?

You can never really get rid of an emotion. As I hope we've shown in the many musical and cultural moments filling this book, doo wop is a link in the long chain of emotional history that is tethered at one end to the very first song sung by man, and at the other to our hopes for the future.

It's a sad but natural truth that many of the original group members are gone. Every once in a while we still see doo wop artists of days past come around on tour. While there are, unfortunately, several pretenders to the throne, you can catch live performances featuring at least one original group member.

Doo wop is still here, and we all still clamor, as we did years ago, to hear these innocent yet beautiful songs. Ever true to its origins, the music touches us because it has never had the quality of being manufactured for the masses or manipulated by technology. Doo wop remains a pure expression of our experience, delivered with the greatest instrument of all: the human voice.

For this closing chapter, I asked some of my friends to share their memories and their feelings about doo wop and this music for many years. I hope you'll enjoy what they have to say.

The heart continues to beat. You can stop a record player, you can unplug a radio, you can finish a piece of cake—but you can never turn off an emotion.

Q&A

What attracted you to the music business?

There was no rock 'n' roll when I grew up, no teenage music. I listened to Hank Williams and Jimmy Reed. But later, hearing groups like the Cadillacs doing "Speedo" was instant identity—it was my music! It was the sound, the approach—a little rebellious, with a sense of urgency.

What do think gives doo wop its timeless appeal?

You didn't need a band or tuxedos. I know that today you see it presented that way, but all you really needed was four or five guys on the corner. It was street music—you didn't need a whole lot. It came from the heart and it gets to the heart.

What are your favorite doo wop songs and groups?

I love the Cleftones and the Dells. I love the Ronettes' "Be My Baby." "Maybe" is one of my favorite songs in the world! "Speedo" by the Cadillacs changed my whole life. The sense of urgency resonated with everything I was going through as a pre-teen. If all those feelings had stayed inside and I had no way to express them, I woulda gotten twisted.

What are your favorite memories of doo wop or the 1950s in general?

Backstage at the Brooklyn Fox, with Chuck Berry, Jerry Lee Lewis, Little Richard, the Everly Brothers, the Ronettes, the Crests—it brought the races together in some way. My best memory is Little Richard's mother telling me, "For a white boy, you have soul—you're part of the family, boy!" It's one of the greatest compliments I ever got.

What do you think is the major difference between the music business today and when you started?

Today the business seems too big to get your arms around. There's a lot of technical advances in equipment that I love, and major differences in transportation, which would have been welcome back in my day. Today, people use synthesizers to create the mood behind your lyrics. But we used vocals—*oohs* and *aahs*. I'm blessed to come from a time when the music was very spontaneous, heartfelt and organic, without a whole lot of formula.

DR. MARTIN LUTHER KING (CENTER) LEADS A PROTEST MARCH

After the McCarthy era showed us we weren't always being told the truth, the next big shock to Americans came in the early and mid-1960s, with the ugly and violent displays of racial intolerance that festered during the peak of the civil rights movement. To those of us living in the cocoons of large, culturally diverse cities, the scenes on TV of racist brutality and of protesters being blasted with fire hoses in parts of the Deep South were a sure sign that all was still not right in much of our country.

The modern African American civil rights movement had kicked off earlier with the landmark Supreme Court ruling in the Brown v. Board of Education case, which made segregation unconstitutional. But in the face of the continued institutionalized prejudice in much of the South, the court's decision had only slowly been enforced. So under the leadership of Dr. Martin Luther King Jr., many activists turned to peaceful methods of civil disobedience: sit-ins, bus boycotts and demonstrations like the 1965 Selma to Montgomery marches. Tragically, we would lose King to an assassin's bullet just three years after the historic Alabama marches.

King was and will always be an inspiring individual, not just to African Americans striving for equality but to people everywhere who value freedom and human dignity. The awareness of racism in America raised by the 1960s civil rights movement represents the most important social development in our nation's recent history. Sadly, the issue of race is one we continue to grapple with today.

Listen carefully and you can hear doo wop echoing in today's music.

Philadelphia who had set the stage for Philly Soul, a latter-day R&B niche pioneered by producers Kenny Gamble and Leon Huff and led by groups like the O'Jays ("Love Train") and the Three Degrees ("When Will I See You Again").

Even if one were to strip out the names, faces and hit songs from Motown, its empty silhouette would bear the same shape as doo wop. Gordy and Smokey took a page from the past when they sought to build a label roster of soulful artists who could bridge the gap between R&B and pop and set both charts on fire. Like doo wop artists, Motown players built their followings on the "Chitlin Circuit"; these were clubs friendly to black performers and audiences, so named for the soul food "chitterlings" (look it up, but don't say I didn't warn you). Motown also fostered a dignified image in their performers that was right out of the doo-wop playbook. When you came to see these guys play, they'd put on a dinner jacket for you. Still do, in fact. That's class.

Doo wop was wholly incorporated into the music of the 1960s—so much so that it seemed to disappear. In truth, it was reincarnated time and time again. Even the doo wop artists who never resurfaced on the charts after the late 1950s have proven to have a remarkable shelf life. Their songs are a bookmark, a place-keeper we use to flip back to a sweet and simple time in our lives.

Listen carefully and you can hear doo wop echoing in new music today. Sometimes we say a son has his father's eyes—the old man may be gone, but we see him in his children.

DION DIMUCCI

Dion DiMucci led Dion and the Belmonts before pursuing an exceptionally successful solo career, which he continues with passion today. Dion was inducted into the Rock and Roll Hall of Fame in 1989.

BRENDA LEE

"Little Miss Dynamite" was one of rock 'n' roll's first female stars, and had many chart-topping hits in the late '50s and early '60s, including the smash "I'm Sorry." Of course, no Christmas is complete without hearing Brenda Lee sing "Rockin' Around the Christmas Tree" and "Jingle Bell Rock." As part of her ongoing projects, she enjoys exploring her gospel roots.

Q&A

What attracted you to the music business?

Well, I started out so young—at seven years of age—that I don't think I knew there was such a thing as the music business! I just knew that I loved to sing and whatever venue I could sing at, that was wonderful. It was the love of singing that was my motivating force. And that's still the case.

What do think gives doo wop its timeless appeal?

I think it falls into the category of any type of music that's timeless and that touches people's hearts and emotions. For music to be timeless, it has to be well crafted, well written and well performed. And doo wop has that. A lot of the doo wop artists were just unique personalities who were not trying to copy the next big thing or the latest fad. And that's why I think there's still a huge audience for that music and for those artists.

What are your favorite doo wop songs and groups?

As trite as it may sound, I like them all—I can learn from everybody. The lead singer of the Brooklyn Bridge—Johnny Maestro?—I love him. I think that era was so fun and so good, and that's why this music is still there.

What are your favorite memories of doo wop or the 1950s in general?

My favorite memory is the camaraderie we had as artists. And the love we had for what we did. Of course, everything has a bottom line. But the artists were so glad to get to do what they loved, everything else was secondary. A lot of us still have that love for the music today.

What do you think is the major difference between the music business today and when you started?

I think it's more of a business now. Not that it hasn't been in the past. Talent used to be the number one requirement, but it's way down the list now. I just see that as the big difference. I don't want to sound like I think nobody's talented now. But it used to be that if you walked into an office and you had to sing, you had to sing—it didn't matter what you looked like or how you dressed. Now, you have to have the whole package. And I'm afraid that there are some talented people who will never see the light of day. But I think the audience knows the difference. It's good to look good, but if you can't follow it up with what you put out there, you can't fool them.

Q&A

What attracted you to the music business?

I grew up in Henderson, North Carolina. We only heard two kinds of music there: hillbilly music and gospel music. But when I was about eight or nine years old, we came to New York, and there was all the excitement of the city and all the different music that you could hear here.

What do think gives doo wop its timeless appeal?

The rawness of the music. It was something anybody could do, but it was when you started harmonizing with other people that you found out if you were good. People gather around you and applaud, that's how you know. Like now, you'll see people skating or drumming in Central Park. They stop a crowd, and that tells them they're doing something that somebody likes!

What are your favorite doo wop songs and groups?

It goes way back to the Spaniels, the Harptones and the Moonglows, even to gospel singers like the Swan Silvertones and the Blind Boys of Alabama. To me, all music comes from gospel. We took doo wop from gospel.

What are your favorite memories of doo wop or the 1950s in general?

My father worked in the restaurant business. His restaurant was in Harlem, on 119th Street and Eighth Avenue, so it was a short walk to the Apollo Theater and enjoying all the professional groups there, which we emulated. We were four guys out of the neighborhood—we called ourselves the Four B's (two Billys, Bobby and me, Benny). We found out we could do harmonies, so we got invited to do school projects. Once, we entered the Amateur Hour at the Apollo, and we won second place.

What do you think is the major difference between the music business today and when you started?

When I started out, we had no profanity in our lyrics. I constantly tell new lyrics writers, "Always write something that someone can pick up a hundred years from now and do again." They understand what I'm saying. I want to hear something that touches the heart; I'm not interested in shock value.

BEN E. KING

Ben E. King is the voice behind cherished Drifters hits such as "This Magic Moment" and "Save the Last Dance for Me." His gorgeous baritone, as heard on the pop/R&B standards from his solo career like "Spanish Harlem" and "Stand By Me," is recognized around the world. Ben E. King continues to tour and his Stand By Me Foundation (www.benekingstandbyme.org) provides scholarships allowing college-age children to major in music.

LENNY COCCO

Lenny Cocco's talent is matched only by his charm, and he is absolutely tireless when it comes to keeping doo wop music honest and active. Lenny is the lead singer of the Chimes and still performs the music he loves.

Q&A

What attracted you to the music business?

Well, my father, Danny Cocco, was a professional accordionist for fifty years. Plus, I used to listen to the doo wop artists played by Alan "Moondog" Freed on the radio. And of course, I would go to Freed's shows, at the Brooklyn Fox and the Brooklyn Paramount. Watching all those performers singing harmonies and doing their dance routines—that had a great effect on me.

What do think gives doo wop its timeless appeal?

It's the words! There's nothing dirty, nasty or suggestive. I always say in my shows that our music is good, clean fun—non-suggestive music

What are your favorite doo wop songs and groups?

My favorite group at first was the Flamingos—my favorite song is "Once in a While," the one I recorded. I love any song that tells a true story: I love you, I miss you, you broke my heart, please come back to me. Nothing dirty, nothing suggestive.

What are your favorite memories of doo wop or the 1950s in general?

There was more respect for other people. We used to hang out until one or two o'clock in the morning, we'd see the old ladies coming home from bingo. It seems like now we've forgotten the word "respect." I have three children and nine grandchildren, and I brought them up with those values.

What do you think is the major difference between the music business today and when you started?

I've been in the business for forty-eight, forty-nine years. When I started, the difference was that there was a lot of payola. The companies had to get the records played. The more they were played, the more it penetrated. Today, it's strictly hits: You have to have talent, you have to be good. This way, it's more accurate. I think it's better now because if you have true talent, it will show.

BOB CROSBY

Bob Crosby is president and CEO of the Vocal Group Hall of Fame (visit www.vocalhalloffame.com) dedicated to helping artists protect, promote and preserve their legacies. He is also an outspoken advocate of the Truth in Music Bill, a law designed to protect artists from identity theft.

What attracted you to the music business?

I've always liked music—I played drums when I was eleven years old. But I found myself better at playing the telephone—as a producer and a manager—than any other instrument! And as a young man in the 1960s, I was attracted to the very powerful music of the time.

What do think gives doo wop its timeless appeal?

Clearly, the vocal group harmony. It doesn't require amplification, instruments or money. Groups were able to sing on the street corners and use their voices as instruments. It was the harmony and the stories the songs told.

What are your favorite doo wop songs and groups?

They're all my favorites! The Vocal Group Hall of Fame is dedicated to honoring the greatest groups in the world. So it would be unfair to pick a favorite.

What are your favorite memories of doo wop or the 1950s in general?

I'm fifty-three years old, so it was the latter part of the 1950s when I got interested in music. Certainly, Elvis had a great influence on me. Being influenced by the great music of the '60s, it took me awhile to discover the great music of the '50s. That was when I realized that it wasn't the first time the music I was listening to had been recorded. So I fell in love with the earlier music, too.

What do you think is the major difference between the music business today and when you started?

The instant access is by far the most distinct difference. The technology in recording today, with pitch-changing abilities and the like, makes it much easier to become a world-famous artist. New artists can make a career out of their talent, whereas earlier you might be talented but have no chance at a career. And with television, artists are able to have visual recognition that was not possible with audio. That's why we created the Truth in Music Bill: A lot of artists don't have that visual relationship with the audience, otherwise they'd be recognizable and it would be much more difficult to impersonate them.

JOE MCCOY

Joe McCoy is an award-winning broadcast consultant. He was vice president and program director at WCBS-FM in New York City from 1981 to 2004, during which time he hired Cousin Brucie. Joe and Brucie continue to work together today on many projects.

What attracted you to the music business?

When I was eleven, I'd listen to Yankee games on the radio, and Alan Freed came on after the games. In high school I sang with a doo wop group, and after high school I was in a band, then went to announcing school.

What do think gives doo wop its timeless appeal?

It's the harmony—the great sounds that come out of four or five people getting together and really feeling the music. If you lived in the city, you were singing under the street lamps, in the boys' bathroom, basements, gyms. Everybody wanted to be the next Frankie Lymon or Dion. It wasn't about money—their whole thing was "Let's get up there and sing and have all those girls swoon!"

What are your favorite doo wop songs and groups?

"I'm So Happy" by Lewis Lymon and the Teen Chords, because it was one of the first songs we sang onstage with my group. "Tell Me Why" by Norman Fox and the Rob-Roys was catchy. For years, I had no idea whether the group was black or white. With baseball players, you had baseball cards, but for recording artists you had no idea. We had no television—just this 45 RPM record going around on the turntable.

What are your favorite memories of doo wop or the 1950s in general?

It was a wonderful time to be a teenager or a kid. We had three baseball teams—plus, it was the birth of rock 'n' roll, and you were the one it was exploding at! You had places to hang out, like soda shops, pizza places and dances after the football games. There was so much going on, you really didn't have to get into trouble or look for trouble. And the records' labels, with all the colors and designs—you could watch them spinning on the turntable, something you can't do with a CD! Or stack them up and watch them flop down on the turntable.

What do you think is the major difference between the music business today and when you started

There was a lot more opportunity to get a record made then. Then, you either were with a record company, or you weren't. Then again, maybe there's a lot more opportunity now, because you've got all these reality shows, or you can make a video and put it on YouTube. People can make their own CDs and sell them at their gigs. But today, it's probably just as difficult to get a label to listen to you as it was back then.

TERRY STEWART

Terry Stewart is the president and CEO of the Rock and Roll Hall of Fame and Museum in Cleveland, Ohio (www.rockhall.com).

What attracted you to the music business?

I was a lawyer, an engineer, a banker…but in my personal life, I was interested in American pop culture: entertainment, music and comics. I got my first records in 1948, went to my first show in 1949—I would rather be around music than anything else. But it wasn't until I was fortunate enough to get a job at Marvel Comics—I was its president from 1989 to 1996—that I recognized that I could do other things.

What do think gives doo wop its timeless appeal?

It's the beauty of the harmony. There's no greater instrument than the human voice. You have great lead singers with great backgrounds and sounds coming out of individuals with no devices. Doo wop was a very unique music that—excuse the expression—struck a chord that seems to be timeless.

What are your favorite doo wop songs and groups?

"Golden Teardrops" by the Flamingos—it has a plaintiveness that I love. "Heart's Desire" by the Avalons—it has some changes where the two lead vocals come together. "Lost Love" by the Superiors, and anything by the Harptones and the Dells.

What are your favorite memories of doo wop or the 1950s in general?

I grew up in the woods in Alabama, and I was more into rockabilly, pop chart stuff, blues. When I came north to go to college in 1963, it happened to coincide with the revival of doo wop. So my great memories are from then, being so flabbergasted by these songs I'd never heard! Plus, all these acts were appearing in New York. Shows lasted all night, groups were still so vital, and this was only ten or fifteen years after their heyday. It was an incredibly exciting time for me.

What do you think is the major difference between the music business today and when you started?

The bad part is that the majors haven't found a way to deal with the technology. There are so few people in the business who have ears. Then, people believed in the music. Now, the business doesn't have the ability to be the clearinghouse it once did. The good part is that individuals can make music themselves now—they can create their own CDs and DVDs, and can support themselves by doing gigs and selling their music there. The buying of music today is optional, and at some point the industry will have to come to terms with that.

Doo Wop Dictionary

THE COOL SCHOOL OF 1950'S LINGO

Actor One who shows-off

Ankle-biter Small child

Ape, go ape State of anger; to erupt in anger

Are you writing a book? Response to someone who is asking too many questions

Back-seat bingo Necking in a parked car

Beehive, B-52 A women's hairdo in which the hair is piled in a conical shape atop the head and held in place with lots of hairspray

Big daddy An older person

Bit An act

Blow To leave (see cut out); to play music; also a drug reference

Boss Wonderful

Bread Cash, money

Cat A cool person, usually a male

Circled Married

Cool Excellent, first-rate; in the know

Cool it Calm down, relax, be quiet

Crazy Especially good

Cream To damage badly, especially a car

Cube A straight, uncool person

Cut out To leave (see blow)

D.A. (Duck's Ass), Ducktail, Duck Butt A men's hairstyle worn by "greasers" in which the hair on the sides is combed back and parted in the middle of the back of the head

Daddy-o A term of endearment, usually in direct reference to another person

Deuce 1932 Ford Model B, the favorite conversion car of most hot rodders

Dig To comprehend; to approve of

'Do Short for hairdo

Drag A bore; something unfortunate

Fake out A disappointing date or meeting

Flat-top A men's hairstyle in which the hair is cut on the back and sides in a close, crew-cut manner and flat across the top

Flick Movie

Flip To become very excited

For real Real, serious

Fracture To cause amusement

Frosted Very angry

Fruit Odd or strange person; annoying person, jerk

Fruity Not appealing

Getting to (first, second, or third) base Various stages of male-female intimacy/making out

Get with it To understand

Goose it To accelerate while driving

Greaser A male who wears his hair with an inordinate amount of pomade grease, usually in a D.A. style

Heavy petting Intimate touching between a couple during necking

Hickey A mark left by an over-zealous suitor leaving a purplish discoloration generally on the neck.

Home run Sexual intercourse

Hot rod, Rod An older car stripped of most nonessential items and fitted with a modified, more powerful engine

In orbit In the know

Jalopy An old and/or battered automobile

Jellyroll A men's hairstyle in which the hair is combed up and forward on both sides and "rolled" together above the middle of the forehead

Kick A good thing

Lay it on me Tell me; give it to me

Like wow Exclamation of being impressed

Make out To neck

(The) Most Deserving of high praise

Nest Hairdo

Nuggets Loose change

Pad One's home

Peepers Eyeglasses

Platter Phonograph record

Pomp Short for pompadour, a type of men's hairstyle in which the sides of the hair are combed back while the top of the hair is fanned forward and curled over itself

Ragtop A convertible car

Real gone Volatile; deeply in love

Session A dance or social gathering; an engagement for musicians, either casual and unrehearsed or of prepared material for recording purposes

Sounds Live or recorded music

Split To leave

Threads Clothing

Tight On close personal terms, good friends

Unreal Beyond comprehension; extraordinary

Wail To drive fast; to play music with intensity and vigor

Watching the submarine races "Serious necking" by a couple in a car parked in a deserted area (popularized by New York DJ Murray the K, who was referring to the young couples who parked along Plum Beach or any secluded locale to make out)

Wedgie A tormenting or teasing prank perpetrated upon a male victim in which the waistband of the victim's underpants is grabbed and jerked upward, pulling the garment into a position very uncomfortable to the wearer

Cousin Brucie's Top 140 Groups

For doo wop lovers, there can never be enough songs or groups. I am asked almost every day to name my favorite doo wop groups. That's a pretty tough assignment…but here goes. How about my Top 140 groups?

Incidentally, I have listed them alphabetically because I really do feel that they all contributed to the great doo wop genre. Now sit back, relax and enjoy your Cuz's Top 140 (and you have my permission to add a few of your own favorites).

1. The Accents "Wiggle Wiggle" 1958
2. Lee Andrews and the Hearts "Tear Drops" 1957
3. The Aquatones "You" 1958
4. Hank Ballard and the Midnighters "Finger Poppin' Time" 1960
5. Dion and the Belmonts "I Wonder Why" 1958
6. Joe Bennett and the Sparkletones "Black Slacks" 1957
7. The Blue Notes "I Don't Know What It Is" 1959
8. The Bobbettes "Mr. Lee" 1957
9. Bob B. Soxx and the Blue Jeans "Zip-A-Dee Doo-Dah" 1962
10. The Blue Jays "Lover's Island" 1961
11. The Cadets "Stranded in the Jungle" 1956
12. The Cadillacs "Speedo" 1955
13. The Capris "There's a Moon Out Tonight" 1961
14. The Castells "Sacred" 1961
15. Cathy Jean and the Roomates "Please Love Me Forever" 1961
16. The Cellos "Rang Tang Ding Dong" 1957
17. The Channels "The Closer You Are" 1956
18. The Chantels "He's Gone" 1957
19. The Chanters "No, No, No" 1961
20. The Charms "Hearts of Stone" 1954

41. The Dominoes "Sixty Minute Man" 1951
42. The Drifters "Honey Love" 1954
43. The Duprees "You Belong to Me" 1962
44. The Earls "Life Is But a Dream" 1961
45. The Edsels "Rama Lama Ding Dong" 1961
46. The El Dorados "At My Front Door" 1955
47. The Elegants "Little Star" 1958
48. The Excellents "Coney Island Baby" 1962
49. The Falcons "You're So Fine" 1959
50. The Fireflies "You Were Mine" 1959
51. The Five Discs "I Remember" 1958
52. The Five Keys "The Glory of Love" 1951
53. The Five Satins "In the Still of the Night" 1956
54. The Flamingos "Golden Teardrops" 1953
55. The G-Clefs "Ka-Ding-Dong" 1956
56. The Genies "Who's That Knockin" 1959
57. The Gladiolas "Little Darlin" 1957
58. The Harptones "A Sunday Kind of Love" 1953
59. The Heartbeats "A Thousand Miles Away" 1956
60. The Hollywood Flames "Buzz Buzz Buzz" 1957

81. The Mello-Kings "Tonight Tonight" 1957

82. The Monotones "The Book of Love" 1958

83. The Moonglows "Sincerely" 1954

84. The Miracles "Got a Job" 1958

85. The Mystics "Hushabye" 1959

86. The Nutmegs "Story Untold" 1955

87. The Olympics "Western Movies" 1958

88. The Paradons "Diamonds and Pearls" 1960

89. The Paragons "Florence" 1957

90. The Passions "Just to be with You" 1959

91. The Pastels "Been So Long" 1958

92. The Penguins "Earth Angel" 1954

93. The Pentagons "To Be Loved Forever" 1961

94. The Platters "Only You" 1955

95. The Quintones "Down the Aisle of Love" 1958

96. The Quotations "Imagination" 1961

97. The Rainbows "Mary Lee" 1955

98. Randy & the Rainbows "Denise" 1963

99. The Ravens "Ol' Man River" 1947

100. The Rays "Silhouettes" 1957

Cousin Brucie Signs Off

Cousins, it's been great taking this journey with you. There's so much creative energy around this music, I feel like I could go for another hundred pages. But I can see by the look in my editor's eyes that we'd better wrap it up for now.

Doo wop music has been in our lives for nearly fifty years, and I think it runs on the fuel of our dreams and emotions. When the creative dream comes alive, as it does in many musical styles, it lifts us all to higher ground. It's common ground, too; one of the pure and simple joys of music is how it brings people together. Every song seems to strengthen the connections among us.

Of course, we have the artists to thank for these gifts. In putting this book together, one thing I really enjoyed was thinking back on all the band stories and appreciating these people all over again. There are groups who are not mentioned here but who absolutely deserve as much respect as we've paid to other doo wop artists. To them—and to you, if I've left out your favorite group—I offer a wholehearted apology. The strength of a chain depends on every link, no matter its size. I sincerely believe that four guys singing around a burning trash can are as important to the progress of music as the Platters singing at Carnegie Hall. My hat is off to all the unsung artists who keep the flame burning on their own street corner.

Thanks for reading and thanks for listening. I'm so grateful to have shared my love of music with you for all of these years.

Jodie, I'm comin' home.

Acknowledgements

Cousin Brucie thanks...

Charlie Nurnberg who has always loved our music and inspired the writing of "Charlie's Book."

My thanks to Carlo DeVito of Sterling for his tireless guidance and support.

My co-writer Rich Maloof for his curiosity, probing mind and talent for making

my personal memories, ideas, approach and writing become

a coherent and entertaining history.

F-Stop Fitzgerald for his organized direction and especially that original phone call.

Karen Jones, her energy, direction and constant encouragement.

David Perry and Jason Cring for design,

Diane Patrick, Teal Hutton and Peter Aaron for their talented team support.

My lawyer Judy Tint for making this whole thing doable.

"Mr. Music", Norm N. Nite for the best information in the biz and

TJ Lubinsky, "the Fountain of Music," for your constant advice and friendship.

Joe McCoy for his belief in me and his many sessions helping to put this whole thing in order.

Neil Sedaka for his friendship both personally and professionally.

Michael Pifferrer and Brian DiNicola of Sirius Satellite Radio for their research skills.

Maria and Chris Angelo, and Jeff Mazzei, three of my dear colleagues and friends

who have always been there for me.

Jerry and Melissa Green of Oldies.Com. for the wealth of music.

Ennio and Michael Ristorante, NYC for the creative space and cuisine.

Les and Nancy Marshak for their ever patient listening and advice.

Especially to my best friend, my wife Jodie for her absolute encouragement, participation

and an occasional lecture on the subject of the moment.

Thank you my darling.

Acknowledgements

Rich Maloof thanks...

Cousin Brucie for sharing his home, his memories and his life story.

His tireless enthusiasm turned a daunting amount of work

into an enjoyable collaboration.

Thank you also to Jodie Morrow for learnin' me on the notion

of complementary schismogenesis.

The team at Band-F Ltd. gave me the opportunity in the first place

and made it all come together in the end—

thank you F-Stop Fitzgerald, Karen Jones, Diane Patrick,

David Perry, Jason Cring, Teal Hutton and Peter Aaron.

Christine M. Corso transcribed hours of interviews accurately, and in record time.

Thanks to Charlie Nurnberg of Sterling Publishing for greenlighting the book

and for his encouraging manuscript reviews.

Lee Knife, HP Newquist and Pete Prown provided interminable,

inane email threads on all things music

which kept me entertained at all hours,

and Erik Wolf put a smile on my tired face from miles away.

Mille grazie to the gentlemen at Ennio & Michael Ristorante in Greenwich Village

for a corner table and a belly full of pasta.

The Good Guys Car Club.

Like many people who write or make music,

I'm indebted to my family and my friends

for standing by whenever I disappear down the rabbit hole.

Without Kris, Daniel and Tess, I'd be a goner.

Bibliography

allmovie Web site, http://allmovie.com

allmusic Web site, http://www.allmusic.com/

Armdur, Neil. "A Love Letter Set to Music," *Smithsonian* magazine, http://www.smithsonianmagazine.com/issues/2004/june/tribute.php

The Beatles: The First U.S. Visit, DVD. London: Apple Corps Limited Under Exclusive License to Capitol Records, Inc., 2003.

Bodanov, Vladimir et al., eds. *All Music Guide: The Definitive Guide to Popular Music.* 4th ed. San Francisco: Backbeat Books, 2001.

The Buck Ram Platters Web site, http://www.buckramplatters.com/

Caldwell, Hansonia. *African American Music—A Chronology: 1619–1995.* Culver City: Ikoro Communications, Inc., 1996.

Classic Motown Web site, Classic Motown & Historical Timeline, http://classic.motown.com/timeline/

The Coasters official Web site, http://www.thecoasters.com/home

Dion DiMucci's official Web site, http://www.diondimucci.com

The Doo Wop Society Web site, http://www.electricearl.com/dws/

Drive-Ins Web site, "Drive-in Indices," http://www.drive-ins.com/dbindex.htm#indxmedia

Floyd, Samuel A. Jr. *The Power of Black Music: Interpreting Its History from Africa to the United States.* New York: Oxford University Press, 1996.

Fisher, Marc. *Something in the Air.* New York: Random House, 2007.

Friedman, Douglas E. and Anthony J. Gribin. *Who Sang Our Songs?* West Long Branch: HarmonySongs Publications, 2003.

Gordon, Alan and Gordon, Lois. *American Chronicle: Year by Year Through the Twentieth Century.* New Haven and London: Yale University Press, 1999.

Gribin, Anthony J. and Matthew M. Schiff. *The Complete Book of Doo-Wop.* Iola: Krause Publications, 2000.

Peter Bacon Hales Web site, "Levittown: Documents of an Ideal American Suburb," http://tigger.uic.edu/~pbhales/Levittown.html

Internet Movie Database Web site, http://www.imdb.com/

Jourdain, Robert. *Music, the Brain, and Ecstasy: How Music Captures Our Imagination.* New York: Harper Paperbacks, 1998.

Bibliography

Kebede, Ashenafi. *Roots of Black Music: The Vocal, Instrumental & Dance Heritage of Africa & Black America*. Lawrenceville: Africa World Press, 1995.

Larkin, Colin. *The Virgin Encyclopedia of Popular Music*, Concise ed. London: Virgin Publishing Limited, 1997.

Levitt and Sons Web site, "Levitt History," http://www.levittandsons.com/LevittHistory.aspx

Little Anthony & the Imperials Web site, "Bio," http://www.littleanthonyandtheimperials.com

The New York Times Web site, http://nytimes.com/

Nite, Norm N. *Rock on Almanac: The First Four Decades of Rock 'N' Roll: A Chronology*. 2nd ed. New York: HarperResource, 1992.

Nite, Norm N. *Rock On: The Illustrated Encyclopedia of Rock 'N' Roll*. Volume 1. New York: Harper Collins, 1982.

Oldies.com Web site, http://www.oldies.com

The Original Ink Spots Web site, http://inkspots.ca/

Radio Hall of Fame Web site, http://www.radiohof.org

Robinson, Jackie and Duckett, Alfred. *I Never Had It Made: An Autobiography of Jackie Robinson*. New York: Harper Perennial, 2003.

Rock and Roll Hall of Fame Web site, http://www.rockhall.com

Songs That Won the War. Volume 2. Hollywood: Stanyan Records CD (15 943), 1992 (5 compact discs).

Southern, Eileen. *The Music of Black Americans: A History*. New York: W. W. Norton & Company, 1997.

The State Museum of Pennsylvania Web site, "Levittown, Pa.: Building the Suburban Dream," http://server1.fandm.edu/levittown/default.html

Surf Ballroom Web site, "History," http://www.surfballroom.com/surf_history.html

Bobby Vee Web site, "Biography," http://www.bobbyvee.net/bio.html

The Vocal Group Hall of Fame Foundation Web site, http://www.vocalgroup.org/

Warner, Jay. *American Singing Groups: A History from 1940 to Today*. New York: Da Capo Press, 2000.

Whitburn, Joel. *Billboard Top 10 Album Charts, 1963–1998*. Menomonee Falls: Record Research, Inc., 1999.

Wynn, Ron, ed. *All Music Guide To Jazz*. San Francisco: Miller Freeman Books, 1994.

Photo Credits

This book would never include so many wonderful images were it not for the dedication of Dave Booth of Showtime Archives in Canada. Many thanks for his cooperation in finding these terrific pictures, album covers, sheet music covers, posters, promotional materials and more. With the exception of the specific photography credits below, all other images were acquired from Showtime Archives.

We also want to thank Renaissance Creative Imagery in Providence, RI, for their expertise in scanning and retouching these images. Our special thanks go to Richard McCaffrey, Judith Wilson, Kimberly Pinto, and Clyde Dunton-Gallagher.

Pages 124-129: © f-stop fitzgerald inc. 2006

Images from Photofest (photofestnyc.com)
Pages 41, 44, 47 (family TV group shot), pg. 47 Milton Berle, courtesy of Showtime, 49, 50/51, 53, 60, 61, 62/63, 66 (2 images), 67, 70, 71, 72/73, 80, 90, 108, 116, 142, 143 (Blackboard Jungle) pg. 143 Rock Around the Clock, courtesy of Showtime, 144/145, 154, 155 (2 images) 156/157, 158, 159, 168, 191, 194, 199, 217, 218, 224, 226, 227, 228, 229, 230/231, 240, 245, 248, 249 (2 images) 254/255, 267, 286, 292, 294, 296, 300, 301, 306/307, 309

Images from BigStockPhoto.com
Pg. 79 © DimensionsDesign. Image from BigStockPhoto.com
Pg. 152 © Jim Parkin. Image from BigStockPhoto.com
Pg. 276 © Lisa F. Young. Image from BigStockPhoto.com

Other Image Sources
Endpapers and TOC: 45s courtesy of Peter Aaron
Pg. 10: Courtesy of Neil Sedaka Music Archives
Pg. 18: Ed Hill
Pg. 313: Dion DiMucci-Courtesy of Showtime
Pg. 314: Courtesy of Brenda Lee
Pg. 317: Courtesy of Ben E. King
Pg. 318: Lenny Cocco: Courtesy of Showtime
Pg; 320: Courtesy of Bob Crosby
Pg. 321: Courtesy of Joseph A. Lenti
Pg. 322: Courtesy of the Rock and Roll Hall of Fame and Museum
Pg. 336: Allison Lucas

Photo IDs: Chapter 1: All courtesy of Showtime Archives
Pg. 23: Scene from Mister Rock and Roll
Pg. 24: Little Joe the "Thriller"
Pg. 33: Scene from Rock, Rock, Rock

"Cousin Brucie" Morrow

"Cousin Brucie" Morrow has worked in the New York City radio market since 1959. A legend in broadcast history, he is the only New York City radio personality to have a street named after him. In 1994 Mayor Rudolph Giuliani proclaimed West 52d Street "Cousin Brucie Way." His amazing on-air journey started at New York's WINS, then a contemporary music station and continued with popular New York stations WABC, WCBS-FM and currently, Sirius Satellite Radio.

It was late one night at WINS where the name "Cousin Brucie" originated. An elderly woman found her way to the station with a different kind of request. She asked, "Cousin, could you lend me fifty cents to get home?" Morrow complied and "Cousin Brucie" was born.

Morrow has been inducted into four Halls of Fame: The National Association of Broadcasters Hall of Fame (2003); Broadcasting & Cable Hall of Fame (1990); the Radio Hall of Fame (1987) and the New York State Broadcasters Hall of Fame (2006). In 1994 he was awarded the Ellis Island Medal of Honor. Morrow serves as Chairman of Variety, the Children's Charity. He made his major motion picture debut in the film Dirty Dancing.

Morrow resides in Manhattan with his wife Jodie and their cat Annie.

Rich Maloof

Rich Maloof has written for CNN, Yahoo!, Billboard, the For Dummies book series, and many others. He is the author of ten titles to date and has been published extensively on health, music, technology, and lifestyle.

Maloof is a front-page contributor to MSN.com (Microsoft Network), where his columns and features appear weekly. Formerly Editor In Chief of Guitar magazine, he has produced dozens of instructional works for musicians as well as the biography of music legend Jim Marshall, The Father of Loud. He lives in Brooklyn, New York.

BAND-F Ltd. Book Packaging

BAND-F Ltd., (www.band-f.com) is a prestigious full-service book-producing company with over twenty years of experience providing top quality editorial, design and production services to the book publishing industry. BAND-F has conceived, written, designed and produced 200 books, with many more in development. BAND-F, has successfully partnered with organizations such as Major League Baseball, USA TODAY, Orvis, A&E Television, ESPN Networks, the National Audubon Society, Frommer's, Fodor's and the Smithsonian Institution.